# For the Love of
# HER Life
## Spring Edition

Compiled by Elizabeth Dyer

Preface by Kit Hinkle

Contributions from the Writing Team at
aNew Season Ministries

Ami Atkins, Jill Byard, Teri Cox, Elizabeth Dyer**Error! Bookmark not defined.**,
Karen Emberlin, Erika Graham, Danita Hiles, Kit Hinkle, Nancy Howell, Linda
Lint, Katie Oldham, Sheryl Pepple, Sherry Rickard, Leah Stirewalt, Lori Reynolds
Streller**Error! Bookmark not defined.**, Bonnie Vickers, Julie Wright, Liz Anne
Wright

**www.anewseason.net**

A Widow's Might

# DEDICATION

You know the walk of solitude after losing your husband. You long for comfort from those who know your ache and can offer the kind of Hope and encouragement that can only come from the Lord through voices of those who have been there.

May you be blessed with our voices as you climb out from this difficult season. May you bless another when she walks in aNew Season, needing comfort during the early stages of loss.

Job 29:13b
Making the widow's heart sing for joy

A ministry of aNew Season.net

# PREFACE

We've talked about placing a devotional book in the hands of widows since the start of A Widow's Might in 2009 and well into the birth of our umbrella ministry, aNew Season. Finally – here it is. When I think of all the ladies not yet online now being able to access these writings, my heart melts.

I picture **For the Love of HER Life**, our book of daily devotions, as a night-table book. One that perhaps someone got for her as a gift of love, knowing how much she is hurting. And at first it sits next to her, unopened.

Until at some point, she's up late at night and needs to hear from other widows. Finally, she'll pull it from her night table to begin reading, letting the comfort of Christ wash over her.

These daily devotionals come straight from our website. They have been proven over the years to bring comfort – the kind that lasts beyond the feel-good hug or reassuring smile, because they bring the comfort of God's Truth.

aNew Season Ministries ministers in the trenches of grief and beyond grief into victorious living through a walk with Christ. For the widow, when it seems no one else understands because they haven't lived it, aNewSeason.net is just a click away and able to minister to her.

We pray that this devotional becomes a way for a widow's friends and family to reach out to her. How many times have I been asked to mentor a widow, speak to her – tell her life isn't over? How many times have a widow's loved ones begged me to let her know that she has purpose and there are healthy ways to deal with grief?

And I do. And so do all the writers on our team.

But what about the widow who hasn't physically come across our path?

This devotional book can be given to her right there when the loss is fresh. It's like giving her a whole network of many women who have successfully navigated grief – women of many ages and situations with one thing in common – the knowledge that Christ is the answer to healing.

When the funeral is finished and everyone has gone home, she will eventually find herself in that place – face to face with her solitude. That's when her friends and family will want this devotional, written by many, to comfort her. As she reads through story after story, she'll get it. She's not alone. Many have walked before her—joyfully.

We've decided to publish these devotionals in three month seasonal cycles. We have enough for a year-long daily devotional, but to publish it in one book would make for a large book unless we abridged the writers' work or made the font so small it would become hard to read.

We pray you or your loved one will be blessed by these writings and hope to engage with you at our conferences or online at anewseaon.net

God bless you!

~Kit Hinkle~

# Prologue

My prayer is that, as you read these daily devotions, you will be encouraged to live life again. You are a beautiful daughter of the King. He has more left for you to experience and give to others in this life. The writers at A Widow's Might/aNew Season Ministries are so blessed with the opportunity to share our writings with you as we journey together on the path of widowhood. Your heart will sing again.

~Elizabeth Dyer~

# Introduction:
# Spring

To the reader of our devotionals for the months of March, April, and May

It is spring. Look around you. Freshness is in the air. You may not have it in your heart just yet, but let the sunshine and new aromas remind you of new life—new hope. Because it's there, even when the reminders of cold winter linger, along with your grief, like the covering of sorrow over what should be the beauty of newness. Melt the sorrow like the late winter snow. Let God's light warm you from the outside in, until you feel the warmth of a spring glow on your heart like the tingle of baby grass beneath your toes. We invite you to walk with us through these months of spring, day-by-day, as we share with you Christ's hope and how it has brought us into our new seasons. We pray you invite Him into yours.

Kit Hinkle and Elizabeth Dyer

# MARCH

### Overcome with Joy!

By Elizabeth Dyer

*I am* **overcome with joy***, because of Your unfailing love,*
*for You have seen my troubles,*
*and You care about the anguish of my soul.*
*Psalm 31:7 NLT*

When was the last time you were overcome? Was it overcome with fear? Guilt? Anger? I often associate being overcome with bad emotions for some reason. When was the last time I was overcome by a GOOD emotion? Overcome with satisfaction? Security? Faith? Joy?

I have trouble remembering the last time I was overcome by joy. Maybe my wedding day, or holding my newborn baby, or seeing my child graduate. But how convicting this verse was when I realized I cannot remember when I was overcome with joy because of something **God** did.

But as I kept pondering this verse, meditating, if you will, I realized something. During those early months of grief, I was full of joy at what God prompted others to do for us -- God saw our troubles and provided for us in such practical ways!

Then memories of my first retreat with the writers of *A Widow's Might* flashed in my head. Totally overwhelmed with joy. I know tears formed in my eyes

1

as I wrapped my arms around these women for the first time.

That is the beauty of meditating on God's Word. I am allowed time to really consider the words and consider what they mean to me. As I first read it, I doubted I ever experienced overwhelming joy. But upon meditating, God brought thoughts to my mind and circumstances that showed this truth. **Meditating takes the focus off myself and onto God's unfailing love.**

*"You have seen my troubles."* The divorce, death, health, financial ruin, rebellious child, lost love, infertility, relationships, addiction, shame, and misunderstanding.

*"You care about the anguish of my soul."* Anguish, distress, suffering, pain, agony, torment.

It doesn't say I was overcome with joy because my troubles were resolved. Or because I got remarried. Or because I was healed. It was solely because the Psalmist knew God saw the troubles and cared. So often I fool myself I can be overwhelmed with joy if only… If only I have the material possessions or have my troubles solved by my definition of solving. Stop. Don't believe that lie from Satan. Satan wants us to think we can only have joy when we have our solutions. God perhaps has other solutions in mind and we don't see the solutions because we keep an inward focus.

I need that today. I need to know that God sees my troubles. I need to know Someone cares. How about you?

*Loving Father, You are the One I can always count on. You are aware of my troubles and stand ready with Your unfailing love to comfort me. Thank You for seeing and caring. Amen*

## March 2

### The Future is Now!

By Kit Hinkle

*But Moses said to God, "Who am I that I should go to Pharaoh, and that I should bring the children of Israel out of Egypt?"*

*Exodus 3:11, NKJV*

Do you ever feel like saying, "Who am I?" like Moses did? Do you ever feel like you're so mired in the day-to-day of managing life without your spouse that it's hard to see beyond it?

Seven years ago I couldn't imagine a future without my Tom. How do I manage to form a plan in my heart while caught up in the job of raising four kids?

"Caught up" is an understatement. I'm sure you've had a lot on your plates, too. When we're left with kids to raise alone and family affairs of the deceased spouse to untangle and manage, the process of life can become arduous and slow. You might have a hard time seeing a vision or purpose beyond the daily mundane.

I bet Moses felt that way. He had been trained as a prince of Egypt only to spend forty years as a simple shepherd. As he tended sheep and wondered about his unused princely skills, I bet he didn't realize the changes going on inside of him.

There are times when I get lost in the tasks of the day and wonder if I can ever see the light at the end of the tunnel. But it's in those tasks where God is working on my future plan, not holding my plan back.

When I raise the boys with a God-focus, the values I want to see in the boys are the same values I need for a healthy future for myself. **By applying**

**those values to them, I'm equally building them in myself.** It's kind of like Moses, in carrying out his duties as a shepherd year after year, he shed his prideful nature and strengthened his surrender to the Lord.

Applying God's values to the kids is strengthening my values and vision for a future. Here are some examples:

- *Writing* – The written word is precious to me and gives me that creative outlet. I've encouraged the boys to begin writing. In turn, they've encouraged me to finish my novel's draft manuscript and take on as many writing projects as I can handle.
- *Travel and mission work* - I want my boys to have travel experiences. I'm adding mission work to the travel because it's so important to build the character of service in the boys.
- *Forethought and planning* - I want my boys to learn how to think ahead and plan for the future, so I talk with my teens a little about our finances. It's gotten me planning my own financial future.
- *Health and Wellness* - I want to keep up with the boys and be strong so I take them with me to work-out several times a week.

Do you see how settling into my role, raising the boys, put into place some of the building blocks for a future? The future beyond my raising boys shouldn't wait. It starts with **how** I'm raising the boys.

*Dear Father, help me in the mundane to see how You are strengthening my values and vision for a future. Open my eyes to see the building blocks I need for this future. Thank You for the beautiful plan for me to fulfill in Your time. Amen*

## <u>March 3</u>

## New Paint

By Bonnie Vickers

*I will give you a new heart and put a new spirit in you;*
*I will remove from you your heart of stone*
*and give you a heart of flesh.*

*Ezekiel 36:26 NIV*

Just before what would become our last family vacation together, my sweet husband gathered his household of girls and announced we would be spending that time at our Texas property, doing, of all things, barn painting! We women were not thrilled. We anticipated something a little more exciting in the middle of a hot July summer.

But we got started, stripping the paint off and removing rotten wood. We worked diligently to rid the walls of old and worn materials. Hours were spent preparing the walls to receive a fresh coat of paint. Rotten wood was replaced. Every inch of bare wood was covered with primer to allow the fresh coat of paint to illuminate renewal.

Finally the day arrived to apply the paint, which brought the barn walls back to life with the artful crafting of the new color on the walls and accents of white to the doors and windows. That discolored shabby barn was transformed.

This barn renewal was so much like my journey through the grief process. Upon entering the third year of widowhood, I sought a new heart and purpose for my deep grief. I had trudged through all the major emotions: denial, sadness, anger, bitterness, disbelief. It was time to replace my "baggage" with renewal, purpose, and a new heart, much like the process of repainting the barn, with three basic steps: strip, prime, and paint!

## Strip Off the Bad:

That first year, a lot had to be "stripped away" from me...denial, anger, bitterness, confusion. There was a bundle of "rotten wood" in my heart. All those plans we had made had to be "sanded away", as well. I knew I had to let go of all that **was** to make room for a transformation. I had to let go of the past.

## Prime Yourself:

The second year was spent "priming" myself. I had to "cover" my heart, thoughts and actions in God's grace. Just as we had to cover every inch of that barn with a primer, so too, I had to allow God to cover every inch of my heart, thoughts, and emotions with His love and grace.

## New Paint:

The third year, I became receptive to receive my new "paint". I began seeking what my purpose would now be in this season of my life. It has taken over three years to arrive at this point, but day by day, I am receiving His "paint" (plan) for my life. I am watching a transformation from despaired widow *to* hopeful widow!-

God has a plan, my Sisters. I have found it impossible to walk this journey and **not** be changed for Him and His glory. My husband would want me to press on, to live, and to live with joy. If I did anything less, it would be a disservice to my husband's memory and to my Christian walk.

*Dear Heavenly Father, Thank You for creating newness in my heart as I move forward in this journey of widowhood. Please create a renewed hope and spirit. My heart aches as I grieve the love I miss. Help me see Your plan and purpose as I seek the change this new chapter will bring to me. Create a new spirit within me Amen*

## March 4

### Covered By His Feathers

By Karen Emberlin

*He will cover you with His feathers*
*and under His wings you will find refuge.*
Psalm 91:4 NIV

Cracker Barrel was always a favorite lunch stop for my husband and me, and the gift shop was as enjoyable as the food! A few months before Don made his journey to Heaven, we stopped for one of those lunches. I spotted a picture and was drawn to it immediately. I like old things and perhaps the old door reminded me of some of the old buildings I used to see in the area where I grew up – it brought back many good memories of our small farm community.

However, for some reason, the verse from Psalm 91 on the picture just seemed to speak out loud to me.

The picture was certainly not a "need" but after a couple more visits to Cracker Barrel over the next few weeks, I decided I would "splurge" and purchase it. I hung the picture in the dining area of our kitchen so I could see it every morning as my husband and I ate breakfast and spent time together in prayer before we started our day.

The economy had taken a toll on our small business and every day seemed to be a challenge. It was easy for me to get discouraged and feel like there was no way out! However, as I looked at the picture each morning, I could just imagine being all cuddled up, embraced in the safety of His feathers and wings. It was so comforting - a place I wanted to stay all day long!

I no longer live in our home where I first hung the picture near our breakfast table. I so miss the morning times we had together and the assurance my husband always gave me that God would take care of us - no matter what! The challenges we faced then are not the same as the ones I face today, but the same picture now hangs in my bedroom as a reminder that God is still here to cover me with His feathers and to take care of me. He even tells me further in this chapter of Psalms that He orders His angels to protect me wherever I go and will give me the best of care if I will only trust Him.

My husband was right, and God is still taking care of both of us - certainly **not in the way I would have chosen but in the way He has chosen**!

Even though my circumstances have changed, how wonderful to know that my God has not changed! He is still there - His feathers still cover me and provide all the safety I need!

*Father, I pray You will never let me forget You are there to take care of me and to protect me. Help me to place all of my trust in You! Amen*

## March 5

## A Time to Cook

By Nancy Howell

I love to cook. I say this because tonight I sit, eating leftover turkey and dressing (defrosted from the freezer) out of a cup, while watching my sons, one eating a peanut butter sandwich and the other a corn dog. What in the world has happened to us? How can the absence of one person in a home turn everything upside down and inside out? Is this the norm for folks that live alone (or are single parents)?

I used to plan meals. We ate around six p.m., without fail, every week-night. I have a collection of cookbooks that are now gathering dust. Every place we'd visit, I'd purchase a locally-inspired cookbook as a souvenir, so you can imagine that my bookshelves are overflowing. My husband enjoyed eating good food, just as he enjoyed life, with gusto, love and appreciation. He loved for me to cook, and I loved to do it.

I would go a week or longer between grocery runs during the first few months. As long as we had milk and bread, we seemed to be able to get by. But after almost four months, I grew tired of not having a dinnertime. We used to sit around, eating and talking about our days. After widowhood, it seemed that the television was on way too much, and tuned into stations I grew to dislike enormously.

The boys were looking to me to lead the household, and, to be quite honest, half the time I didn't have a clue. I talked a good game, smiled and assured them that "I've got this," while my heart and brain were telling me otherwise. You'd think something as easy as re-establishing dinnertime would be a no-brainer.

But there was a glaringly-empty spot at the table. I kept my position, strategically placed closest to the kitchen, so I can grab things as needed. The boys, however, have rotated spots. One took over Daddy's spot, across from me, and the other moved to his brother's vacated spot. We miss the master of conversation, the guy that never lacked for things to say, who was never quiet unless his mouth was full. I pale in comparison, and I'm sure not as interesting to his sons. The empty spot at the table and in our hearts is why our dinnertime consists of sandwiches and defrosted meals in cups.

I think if we can get back into the groove of a more normal eating pattern, we may begin to feel better about things in general. I'm ready to begin scanning my cookbooks for new creations.

There really is something about gathering around a table. It's a time for laughter, conversation, and nourishment for both body and soul. With it, you can gaze lovingly (or laughingly) into your family member's eyes and connect. Without it, the family (at least this one) is just existing, not nourishing itself.

Well, the buck stops here. Tomorrow I make a real grocery list. One that includes fruits, fresh veggies, and maybe a special beverage. I pledge to have a dinnertime plan in place. Now if I can just remember what fresh produce looks like!

*Father in Heaven, I am so glad you understand these changes in our lives. Help us take little steps in order to take care of ourselves and our families. Nourish our souls as we nourish our bodies. Amen*

## March 6

## It Can!

By Erika Graham

Most of my life I believed God was faithful through the bad times, the storms of life. I believed in my head this was true, and I saw with my eyes, through others' difficult circumstances, that it looked true. But, without my own severe storm, without that first-hand knowledge, I'm not sure now my heart truly believed it.

Then, something terrible happened in our life, thrusting us into the deepest storm I'd ever known. When my head didn't understand and my eyes could see nothing, I had only my heart left. That's where God met me; broken, bewildered, blind, and on my knees, pouring out my heart in a storm so severe, I wasn't sure we could survive.

It's been over four years since our catastrophic storm hit...the day my beloved husband journeyed to heaven by taking his own life.

Death is a kind of storm that no one can ever be fully prepared for, and suicide takes it to a dimension of intensity not many understand. *It can* easily create destruction and devastation for all. *It can* turn everything you believed inside-out and upside-down. *It can* give Satan such a foothold, and *it can* thrust those left behind into such a shock, there's the potential for no return.

*It can!*

The "Suicide Storm" is brutal and leaves a mess. It left an ugly, scary mess, and far more questions than answers.

So, how have we survived?

What's allowed us to move forward, to heal, and to even grow?

Who thwarted Satan's plan of destruction?

**God did!**

Because of the Almighty Father, we moved from suicidal death being the "*it can*" storm of destruction, to the "**God did**" story of restoration. My children and I are a walking, breathing testimony to God's faithfulness through a horrific storm!

God doesn't tell us life is fair or easy, or that we won't suffer or die. In fact, He warns us we **will**, so we better get prepared. Preparedness comes from knowing God intimately, hiding His Words deep in our hearts, and trusting that He is totally and completely in control during every moment of every day.

Then in the midst of any storm, *it can* becomes **God did**!

~*It can* be so tough, **God did** show us He's stronger. *Psalm 105:4*

~*It can* be really sad, **God did** show us He understands deep sadness and He will be near the broken-hearted. *Psalm 34:17*

~*It can* be scary looking, **God did** show us He creates beauty. *Ecclesiastes 3:11*

~*It can* be overwhelming, **God did** show us with Him all things are possible. *Matthew 19:26*

~*It can* be long term, **God did** show us He has gone ahead to prepare for us. *Deut. 31:8*

~*It can* be a hard road, **God did** show us that He has us right where He wants us. *Psalm 16:8*

~*It can* be devastating, **God did** show us He will heal us and bind up our wounds. *Psalm 147:3*

~*It can* be ugly, **God did** show us that ugly stuff will grow us. *1 Peter 5:10*

~*It can* be frustrating, **God did** show us that trusting Him is the only way. *Proverbs 3:5*

~*It can* be hopeless, **God did** show us hope is not found here, but in our eternal victory and sealed place in heaven with Him. *Jeremiah 29:11*

*Father God, thank You for being so faithful to me in the midst of such a tragic, horrific storm. Thank You for Your promises strewn throughout Scripture. Lord, Your word has every answer I need. Help me see Your fingerprints everywhere. Move me from the "it can" ugly stuff to the "God did" promises and assurances. In Your precious and matchless name, Amen.*

## March 7

## God is Sovereign, I Am Not!

By Ami Atkins

*For I consider that the sufferings*
*of this present time are not worth comparing with the glory that*
*is to be revealed in us.*

*Romans 8:18 ESV*

As the jet ascended, Chicago's city lights overtook the night, light saturating the terrain. It engulfed the darkness, and I marveled at its radiance. Cars became pin pricks in the distance. A clearly designed grid, created by human minds, glowed against the black sky. From above, there was order in neat squares.

To the right I could still see the rise of giant skyscrapers. Straight ahead the light ended abruptly;

Lake Michigan was ink against the line of fire. It was an ethereal beauty, a peaceful calm, far removed from the congested streets, the homelessness, the hundreds of thousands of stories, the real-life struggles.

Too soon though, the city's brilliance receded into the distance. And there was darkness. How feeble was the light of much smaller towns. Light no longer engulfed the night.

But at thirty thousand feet, I understood that darkness existed only in pockets. The inky patches didn't frighten me because I could tell they didn't last forever. Other cities, other towns slid into view. The light of one city emanated like spokes of a wheel, illumination concentrated at a central hub. Over other cities, light sprawled without any discernible pattern but still in magnificent contrast to the night.

From my vantage point, light interrupted darkness, darkness interrupted light, a constant ebb and flow. It reminded me of life- joy mingled with sorrow, sorrow mingled with joy.

"I could stay here, removed from the grit and messiness. I could stay in the place where I can see the grand design."

Then my thoughts funneled to a single truth. God is sovereign. I am not.

He is above all things. He understands all things. He is in control over all things. He sees the beginning and the end, the dark patches and the light.

Unlike a pilot, He doesn't merely know the final destination, He sees the entire journey at once. I cannot claim to fully understand, but I know He guides all things. Through grief, I've learned to mine the depth of God's sovereignty, and I've found it immensely comforting. God was sovereign over my husband's death.

A high view of God's sovereignty keeps me grounded in the reality that nothing could have thwarted His will.

Likewise, though I long for an aerial view, God's mercy limits my sight to the ground-level path in front of me.

Perhaps if I knew the future I would run away, afraid to face what is to come. Praise God I cannot see the aerial view!

At ground level, He teaches me to trust Him. **The One who sees the final city, will lead me safely to it.** In His goodness He gives "seas of ink". And In His goodness He gives "cities of magnificent light".

*Lord, You are sovereign. You are in control over all things, and no one can thwart Your plan. You are transcendent, but You are also personal. Thank You that my Savior is intimately acquainted with grief, and walks through darkness with me. You are radiant light. You are joy. I rest here today. Amen*

## March 8

## The Upward Kick

By Kit Hinkle

*I press on toward the goal for the prize*
*of the upward call of God in Christ Jesus.*
*Philippians 3:14 ESV*

Do you wake up every morning feeling like you have nothing significant to look forward to? Have you lost that kick in your step? I promise, sister, you can get it back. I plodded through that first year after losing my husband Tom, wondering if I would ever feel joy again. Seven years later I have a spring in my step again. As God heals, you go from having the wind knocked out of your sails to being engaged again with life—engaged with an excitement about the future!

### How did the Kick in Your Step Feel?

First, step back and examine how it felt to have a kick in your step. Perhaps the last time you had one was when you were married. You may have squabbled with your husband over daily burdens, or perhaps you peacefully moved through troubles together. Either way, there was a fire in you. You knew the two of you would get through life together. Deep down, you assumed you had him to grow old with. You had something to look forward to.

### Look Forward to Something Else

The next step is to look forward to something else. I imagine the apostle Paul and his selfless journey without a wife as a companion—telling the world about the kingdom of God. He longed for what awaited him in Heaven, but he looked forward to the here-and-now as well.

Now, I've heard it said many times to widows—*you can look forward to that glorious day when we all stand before the Lord.*

Of course, that's true. But ...

When you are widowed, and many of your friends are in married-life mode, it's difficult to desire your future joy when compared to their present happiness. Looking forward to the afterlife in order to feel whole again may not immediately put a kick back in your step. But over time, little by little, it can happen.

## Paul's Example

Every day, Paul chose to be used for God's purposes. In Philippians 3:14 he tells us to aim daily to be more Christ-like, all while we look toward the prize of the upward call of Christ (being in God's presence in Heaven). How can we do this too?

The third step to getting our kick back is to take time to spiritually grow so that the grief is resolved to where our focus is on the Lord, not on our loss. There are resources on our website that can walk you through the healing Christ offers. He can help you let go of your claim to your past season and begin anew.

While you are trusting the Lord will heal, try new interests. Don't wait. Read, join a book club, begin a few courses, or take on jobs that will help you figure out your goals.

In my first year after losing Tom, I spent some time writing. It was something I had done for many years, but now I had a great deal to write about. My pastor's wife also invited me to help market her chiropractic business. I didn't think marketing was up my alley, but I found that being involved with the Chamber of Commerce and getting out in public was not only comfortable, but fun. It balanced the introspective writer in me.

At the time, I didn't know where the Lord would take those activities. Now, I write and speak in public to minister to women.

The more I use the interests and gifts He's laid on my heart, the less I dwell on my grief. The healing is overcome by my excitement for the future—both now, as I grow more Christ-like, and for Heaven.

*May the Lord help you find your interests and gifts, Sister. May He enliven your spirit with a sense of a bright future with endless possibilities. God bless you!*

## March 9

## Morning Coffee

By Linda Lint

> *Satisfy us in the morning with Your steadfast love.*
> *Psalm 90:14 NRSV*

He - a certified, card-carrying, morning person. Me - not so much.

While my husband happily engaged in his morning routine, I clung to the covers just as long I could. As I slowly came awake, I could hear the sound of water running, rustling clothes, food pouring into the dog dish and finally his voice "Linda, time to get up!".

By the time I made my way to the kitchen table, he was waiting for me, with a smile and a fresh cup of coffee - prepared to just the right temperature and exactly the way I liked it. He had learned early on that his bride required coffee first thing!

As I think back on those mornings, I realize how much love was there between us. He accepted me as I was. He had no requirement for a put together, wide awake Linda. My beloved was simply glad to be with me and share the time together. And I was comfortable just being myself.

We shared so many conversations over morning coffee. Sometimes we were able to sit for one or two hours talking. Other days our schedules required a shorter visit. Our love for each other grew over the years because we took that sacred time in the morning to be together.

Then came the morning I noticed his hand shaking while holding his cup and realized that he had

had a stroke. Sadly it was the last "morning coffee" that we shared. He was not able to return to our home.

I embarked on a journey with him that included the hospital and care center and finally saying that last farewell early one morning before the sun rose - and coffee for one.

Now I have my morning coffee as I sit at the same kitchen table. Although I am physically by myself, I am not truly alone. God is right here with me. My God, who is now my husband, awaits me each morning, accepting me as I am. He even arranged for me to have one of those fancy single serve coffee makers, so I can have my first cup just as soon as possible!

We have wonderful conversations, and I have come to treasure our time together. My love for Him has grown during our sacred time together, and He has shown me so much. It is often during these visits that He sends me the inspiration for what I share here.

Each day continues to be a challenge as I adjust to life alone. I have come to realize that just as it took me a while to adjust to sharing my life with another, it will take a while to adjust to this one. I go into it each day knowing that God is by my side and will satisfy me with His steadfast love - as only He can.

*Dear Father: In thanksgiving I come to You this day. I praise You for Your steadfast love and Your acceptance of me just the way I am. I will continue to rely on You for guidance and direction through the upcoming days. You are indeed enough! Amen*

## March 10

### Stay in the Game*

By Sherry Rickard

*And when the fowls came down upon the carcasses, Abram
drove them away.*
Genesis 15:17 KJV [Please read Genesis 15:1-17]

My daughter has played field hockey for the last four years. This game is the perfect combination of feminism and strength. Before the warm ups and games, everyone is getting their hair braided with pink ribbons. Even their uniforms are kilts.

During the game, sometimes the sticks of the opposing players hit each other, which causes their knuckles to "clang" against the opponents' sticks. The pain, like a tuning fork, runs from hand to elbow. Field hockey game clocks don't stop. You will see these girls continue running and flinging their hand in the air to make the throbbing stop until they have full control of their fingers again. The player keeps going, just shakes it off, and the game continues.

As I think about this particular injury, it is much like the grief walk. You are hurt and it throbs throughout your body. You can just let the throb go on and on and do nothing, or you can push through, shake yourself, and tell yourself to go on. You have to make yourself "stay in the game" of life. You have to keep on, keepin' on. God has this; but you are called to do some of the work. Just like in the verses of Genesis 15:1-17. God wanted to bless Abram; but Abram had to drive away the birds. God could have done it Himself, but he called Abram to do his part.

21

So, what are you called to do? You are asked to get up each day; eat healthy; exercise; and keep on going. If you are doing well; everything else falls into place. If you have children; they will follow your lead. You have to do your part. That is different for each person. It feels good sometimes to be the saddest person in the room; but that is not healthy, nor does it glorify Christ.

What if you haven't been doing that? What if you have fallen into the habit of being sad, and it is not a clinical condition or early in your grief journey? Do better - starting now! Pledge to yourself and your Savior that tomorrow will be a better day...and DO IT! Get up and meditate on God's word; make yourself smile; brush your teeth; make a doctor's appointment; wear clothes that make you feel pretty; fix your hair (or get a haircut); get a manicure; listen to music that makes you smile; pick one area of your life and make it orderly. Every day, add another thing and before you know it; you will feel better.

You have to "stay in the game" and you are called to do your part. You want your life to honor Christ and to honor the life of your husband. Would he want you to lie in bed and cry all day? Would he want you to withdraw from life? The answer is NO! Smile and shine your husband's testimony - honor the life he lived by living well. Honor the life Christ has given you by living well for Him.

This all sounds easy, but it's not. You have to start with your head and your thoughts and then you have to take action. You can do this! Shake it off! Stay in the game!

*Dear Lord, Thank You for placing people in my life to remind me to "stay in the game". Thank You for loving me through this. I will do better and I will purpose to glorify You in my life. Amen.*

\* Author's Note: There are times when medication is needed to help people get through because of a clinical condition and, in those times, one should seek medical advice and adhere to that advice.

## March 11

### Arise

By Teri Cox

*Arise, shine, for your light has come,*
*and the glory of the Lord has risen upon you.*
*Isaiah 60: 1 ESV*

I used to do something that I called, "alphabeting God". I actually picked the idea up from a pastor friend of mine, who recited one of his alphabet praises to God as part of a sermon one Sunday, many years ago. It used to be a way for me to communicate with God in my quiet times. At our recent aNew Season Widows Retreat in Myrtle Beach, I was reminded of it once again.

As I taught and interacted with the ladies at the conference and helped lead worship, I was reminded of the power of one word describing God in so many ways.

He is Awesome, Beautiful, Caring, Dependable, Everlasting, Father, Gracious....You get the idea. "Alphabeting God" is a way of singing His wonder and praises.

Watching the sisters who attended our retreat inspired me. So many broken but healing widows led me to places that I had not been in a while, on my own grief journey. I remember the days when all I could do was breathe and anything after that was just bonus effort. I remember the deafening silence and loneliness that ravaged me.

"It will get better,." I remember people saying that and not believing it. But, it will! Why, because God is faithful and He has not forgotten you! You are still loved and special and chosen, by the maker of the universe. He ADORES you!

Being in such a beautiful location and watching all of the participants on their own road to healing, sharing with others around them and making new bonds with sisters who get it, reminded me that God is an:

**A**mazing
**R**estorer
**I**n
**S**plendor
**E**ternal

He is Honorable, Indescribable, Just, King, Lover of my soul, Majestic, Nobility, Warrior, eXalted, Yearning for you, Zion's Redeemer and He has been waiting for you.

Run to Him.
Fall into Him.
Love Him.
Give Him yourself; completely.

He will help you ARISE. He will trade beauty for ashes and mourning for joy.

*God, refresh me as I live, move, and breathe. Comfort me and help me arise and be renewed through You. In Jesus name, Amen*

## March 12

## The Freedom to Say, "No, Thank You."

By Liz Anne Wright

*There was also a prophet, Anna, the daughter of Penuel, of the tribe of Asher. She was very old; she had lived with her husband seven years after her marriage, and then was a widow until she was eighty-four. She never left the temple but worshiped night and day, fasting and praying. Coming up to them at that very moment, she gave thanks to God and spoke about the child to all who were looking forward to the redemption of Jerusalem.*

*Luke 2:36-38 NIV*

I have always been fascinated by Anna and her small, but pivotal, role in this unfolding drama that is our Lord's start in life. *How* could she stay devoted to God, constantly in the temple, for all those years?

More recently, I have been touched by her widow status. Anna had been a widow a long, long, *long* time. And because she was, she was able to *be there* in the temple when the Lord was dedicated.

Recently, several of my widow sisters have stepped forward into love again...dating, getting engaged and re-marrying. I am *over the moon* in my excitement for them. They have found great guys, in line with God's calling on their lives, and have not been afraid to plunge into the waters of loving again.

But...while I am thrilled for them, I am equally certain that this course is not for me. Not now...maybe not ever.

And that's okay. I know it's okay because of Anna.

Dedicated simply to the Lord's service, no distractions in her path, she prayed and fasted and went about the Lord's business. That, to me, sounds like Heaven on earth!

I bet she was the go-to gal for prayer concerns, and kept her friends, family, town, and nation bathed in prayer. I bet she could sit and **listen** to the Lord for hours, and knew His voice as clearly as her own. I bet she had sweet, solitary worship, hands raised above her head, as she told her Lord how much He meant to her.

Maybe it's because my life is so crazy now that this sounds appealing. I know I often long for simplicity and more oneness with God, oneness that I especially long for since I am without my sweet husband. Maybe it's because I long to be able to be singularly focused on Kingdom things, not on the minutia of life on earth. Perhaps it's simply that I am tired and long for the rest that only my Savior provides, and I long to listen more closely to His voice.

Whatever the reason, this is my season...God-ordained, just as much as my sisters who are again dating and married. God has purpose and meaning in both paths, and by His grace, we can be fulfilled in both.

I pray that as you consider whether to date or to remarry, you lean on our loving Lord to make those decisions. He has all the answers we need.

*Father God, I pray that You guide me on my journey of singleness, dating, and remarriage. I pray that You help me to know which path is best for me now and always, and I pray that I can walk boldly forward to serve You, single or married, just as You would have me do. In Jesus' Name, Amen.*

## March 13

## Dressing for the Season

By Jill Byard

> *Clothe yourselves with the full armor of God*
> *so that you may be able to stand*
> *against the schemes of the devil.*
>
> *Ephesians 6:11 NET*

Do you remember as a child being bundled up in winter gear? Dressed so snug that it was hard to bend knees and elbows while playing in the crisp cold winter air. All of our layers restrained our movement.

That mummy-like walk might be acceptable for the winter season but it isn't working well in everyday life. In the twelfth chapter of Hebrews we are called to "throw off everything that hinders". Shame, disappointment and guilt do not fit anymore. They are clothes of my past. They impede movement and responses.

The winter clothing with all its bulk does serve a purpose, but I have found something that fits even better.

**I have come to realize the Armor of God draped with a layer of grace is the best tailored outfit in my spiritual wardrobe.**

I need to be vigilant about checking to make sure my Armor of God is in working order and ready for battle.

- The belt of truth needs to be wrapped around me snugly so all my armor can remain in place and I am continually protected.
- The helmet of salvation reminds me I have been bought with a price and the words of the

enemy will not take root in my brain any longer.

- The breastplate of righteousness is essential in helping me remember His righteousness covers me and my past has been forgotten.
- My sandals of peace provide traction when I encounter rough terrain. Harsh words, unfair expectations and unpleasant people make for slippery conditions and my sandals of peace are vital equipment.
- My shield of faith deflects the flaming arrows of the enemy and keeps shame and guilt from lingering in my closet.
- My sword of the Spirit (which is the word of God) is used daily to slay every trick the enemy tries to use to knock me off the path God has placed me on.

Sweet friends, as widows we have to be prepared and intentional about wearing our armor of God. It is an essential part of our wardrobe; without it we are vulnerable. As we work daily towards being a warrior, remember God always drapes our efforts with His grace. He honors our diligence and He knows the placing of every one of our footsteps.

*Dear Lord, I am so thankful You know our every footstep. Help me remember how important it is to wear my armor every day. Give me courage to be intentional in preparing for my battles. I want to honor Your name above all else. In Your Mighty name, Amen.*

## March 14

### Whose Plans?

By Kit Hinkle

"So what about a career?" my friend asked. I had just gone through explaining what I wanted in my future after raising boys. I figured I was on the right track. To her, something was missing.

My friend wanted to see me nail down my career. "You're a writer, so publish," she said. "Your manuscript is drafted, finish it. Start marketing yourself." She wanted to see me out there, getting more articles written, posting more on my blog and social media.

I puzzled over our differences. I thought it was enough to know a general direction ten years out and that I was building my writing skills at my own pace. She wanted me to have a game plan. Is either of us right?

My hunch is there is something to gain from both perspectives, but the Lord has each of us in a unique place in life. **Only staying in tuned with God's direction can give you assurance you're taking the right direction.** My friend has no children so her career is her focus in life. It's how she interacts and meets new people in her life whom she can minister to and help along the way.

I've been in the career world before. I tend to approach career with single-minded focus and attention, much as I approach raising my children. I could dive in and plan a future career now, but I know my limitations. My focus would move away from where God is asking me to place it—on the boys.

I think about how odd I must seem to the world, not marching to their drum. In this working mom, working-woman-magazine-inspired culture, my choice goes against the grain.

Joshua's men went against the grain of the world after they crossed the Jordan and came across the city of Jericho. They were told by an angel of God that the city was to be theirs, but wouldn't be handed to them. They had to be courageous and obedient to get it.

God tells us we are to handle what He's put before us, whether it's raising kids or managing a career, and He will take care of us, but we need to be obedient first, even to the point of staying in a less-than-glamorous role for now.

The angel's instructions to Joshua's men seemed crazy to the world (it may have even seemed crazy to them). Rather than fight Jericho dead on, they were to march around the walls in silence and blow horns at Jericho. Imagine the trust Joshua's people had in God to do such a thing. Did they really believe God would give them the city after marching and blowing horns?

Do you really believe God will deliver you out of your circumstances if you trust and obey Him?

We are asked to do tough things as widows, with gnawing feelings that we're not taking care of our own plans. If you are listening and feel the Lord is encouraging you to stay at the current job, trust Him that He has your future provided for.

I'm grateful for my friend's questions, though. She stretched me to think more carefully about the future.

## March 15

## Who Is Responding?

By Danita Hiles

The place: Store dressing room....two nights before a family vacation.

The players: One exhausted mama, one hormonal high-schooler and one hungry third-grader.

The scene: Trying to find a few key clothing items to take on the upcoming vacation.

The mood: Stress!

Stress between sisters, stress with the shopping experience, stress coupled with feelings of failure that this should have been done sooner, stress over the struggles with sizes and prices, stress of peer pressure and expectations. Not to mention the anticipation of yet another single-mom trip and all the details which that entails.

I sat on the floor in the middle dressing room, a daughter on either side of me in their own rooms. Tensions were high and things were not fitting or too pricey or simply just wrong for what we needed.

Needless to say, our collective "manna" for the day had long since been depleted.

We really should have all been home in comfy pjs, eating soup and listening to something relaxing.

Instead, I sat under the unforgiving fluorescent glare fitting-room lights, hoping for a fashion miracle to emerge from either side of me.

Siblings with short fuses quickly began to take out their frustrations on each other...and then on their mama. Does that ever happen in your house? I was headed down the slippery slope of a first-class mama-meltdown when I heard it.

A voice from above.

Now, before you get all excited and super spiritual, it wasn't the Lord...you know the voice, it was the lovely lady from the store P.A. system.

"Team members," her silky tones inquired, "Assistance is needed in the Ladies department...who is responding?"

And again she calmly asked, "Assistance is needed in the Ladies department...who is responding?"

Funny how I've heard that expression hundreds of times during my shopping adventures but this time it was personal: Assistance is needed...who is responding?

Sitting in a dressing room, full of frustration, who is responding?

Faced with pouty children and sulky sales clerks, who is responding?

Feeling sorry for myself and my single-mom life, who is responding?

Is it a tired, cranky mama who just wants to get home?

Or is it the Jesus-loving girl who wants to be a blessing and shine her light, in spite of the current drama life is dishing out?

There are an awful lot of things I can't control.

But **I can choose how I respond.**

Colossians 3:12-13 is the best dressing room advice ever: *'Therefore choose to clothe yourself with compassion, kindness, humility gentleness and patience. Bear with each other in forgiveness. And over all this, put on love.'*

Sitting there on the dressing room floor, I came face to face with my own ugly attitude. Sigh.

It was time for one tired, cranky mama to step aside. This Jesus-girl has got to try some new things on.

I reached up for some compassion and put it on, pulled over some humility and wrapped it around, grabbed some patience and slipped it on for size and covered it all with a giant cloak of love.

And guess what? When mama's attitude changed, the stress disappeared.

Funny how that works.

Never did find the perfect outfits for vacation.

But it just didn't seem to matter anymore.

What about you....when life gets messy, who is responding?

*Lord, in this crazy journey called life, help me to stop and call out to You first. Help me respond with wisdom instead of just reacting to the situation. I love You, Lord. Amen*

## March 16

## It's Heaven Because Jesus is There!

By Ami Atkins

The other day I came across a sentence written in the margin of my Bible.

**"Behold the glory of Jesus!"**

It was dated January 27, 2013.

I stopped in my tracks, stunned. I had no recollection that I wrote it, but there it was in my handwriting.

The date was merely two days after the death of my husband. No wonder I don't remember the words! But the day itself is extremely vivid.

*It was the first worship gathering after Jon died. Though I was still in shock, I was compelled to be with the church. Grief crushed me like a freight train, but I had to go. God's grace was tangible. The Holy Spirit's presence was so powerful, almost physical.*

*I was surrounded by so many who loved me. That day I knew my church was family. Every person wanted to bear the weight of sorrow with me. Tears flowed freely. No one seemed to want to leave. My husband was also deeply loved.*

I scanned down the page of my Bible, trying to recall the sermon. I don't remember it, but somehow, "behold the glory of Jesus" broke through the fog.

As I read the passage my pastor must have preached, **I landed on some tough stuff.**

*"Do not lay up for yourselves treasures on earth, where moth and rust destroy and where thieves break in and steal, but lay up for yourselves treasures in heaven, where neither moth nor rust destroys and where thieves do not break in and steal. For where your treasure is, there your heart will be also." (Matthew 6:19-21) ESV*

And then I remembered. When I heard those words two days after my greatest fear became reality, I thought *"Yes, my heart is heaven. My treasure is there because that's where Jon is."*

Somehow I think "behold the glory of Jesus" was the response I wanted to have.

But at two days, my most cognizant thoughts were, "I just want him back, or God, You could just take me there too? Please." I longed for heaven because Jon was there.

Over time, I've pondered "treasure" often. To treasure something is to value it highly. An ultimate treasure is what we value most highly, that which takes precedence over all. It's the thing that captures our attention and holds sway over our emotions.

I've reached some difficult conclusions. **Jon cannot be my ultimate treasure, but Jesus must be.**

It's tempting to remember my husband through only rose-colored memories. He *was* wonderful, but he was also fallible. He loved me, but he also failed me, as I did him. Yet Jesus never fails.

Now let me clarify, to treasure Christ above all does not mean I love Jon any less. But it does mean **I want my love for God to be so exponential**, that love for Jon seems paltry in comparison.

That's hard thing to hear. I know. It's a hard thing to write.

I've found that the more I know God, the more I treasure Him. The more I dwell on the realities of the death and resurrection of Christ, the more **I am mesmerized by Him**. I have learned what it is to long for Jesus.

When I was crushed by a freight train, when I longed to go where Jon was, even then my soul grasped for truth. My emotions screamed the opposite, but the Holy Spirit broke through the fog.

"Behold the glory of Jesus!"

Heaven isn't heaven because Jon is there. **It's heaven because Jesus is there.**

## March 17

### Whatever It Takes

By Sheryl Pepple

**Whatever It Takes** – words that can either haunt me or inspire me depending on where my emotions are when the words come to mind. It is a commitment I made to God exactly thirty days *before* my husband was killed. I was at a Leadership conference for church and business leaders when they brought out a clay pottery vessel. The vessel represented us, as God made us, but was then shattered into pieces representing the brokenness we experience in this world. We were each handed a broken piece and encouraged to write whatever was on our hearts. I vividly remember the fullness in my Spirit that day, as I wrote…**Whatever It Takes.**

Scripture warns us, there will be a cost to follow Christ.

*Then he said to them all: "If anyone would come after me, he must deny himself and take up his cross daily and follow me. For whoever wants to save his life will lose it, but whoever loses his life for me will save it.*

*Luke 9:23 NIV*

*In fact, everyone who wants to live a godly life in Christ Jesus will be persecuted.*

*2 Timothy 3:12 NIV*

As a widow, I am more aware of the cost. I am more aware of the pain, God endured by sacrificing His Son on the Cross.

I am more aware, I have to deny myself in order to follow him. I have to deny my frequent desire to surrender to my emotions, in order to walk by faith and honor our God.

I am more aware of the persecution of our faith; more sensitive to the constant push in our daily lives - to rely on ourselves, to blame God, to become our own god.

I am more aware, I need to be obedient in the little things, so I can be trusted with the bigger things.

Those three simple words – **Whatever It Takes** - are now woven into the very core of my being. God has brought me to a place where I know and love Him in a way that has brought about a whole new level of surrender. It has been at great cost, but it has also brought *tremendous gain*. Today there is less of me, more of Him.

There are times when I slip back into my old way of thinking, but He always brings me back to my purpose, to glorify Him.

Ladies, He is faithful, He will supply all of our needs. My prayer for each of us is the same as the one Paul prayed for us long ago:

*Philippians 1: 9 -11 NIV*

*And this is my prayer: that your love may abound more and more in knowledge and depth of insight, so that you may be able to discern what is best and may be pure and blameless until the day of Christ, filled with the fruit of righteousness that comes through Jesus Christ-to the glory and praise of God. Amen.*

## March 18

## Transforming Power

By Lori Reynolds Streller

> *But the fruit of the Spirit is love, joy, peace, patience, kindness, goodness, faithfulness, gentleness and self-control.*
>
> *Galatians 5:22-23 NIV*

Being a widow is not exactly what we had planned for our lives, is it? Being dealt the "BIG W" card has really shaken things up. So many things are vastly different in our lives without our husbands. Practically every aspect of our world has been altered.

Oddly, as I am learning to accept this new title, I realize it isn't just that *my life* has drastically changed; it is that *the innermost part* of me is shifting as well.

Listen, I've had a love affair with our God since the age of 14. He has been constant and patient towards me. My devotion has ebbed and flowed throughout the decades. Regretfully, I have spent some seasons distancing myself from His righteousness, and thankfully, I have spent many seasons running full speed into His open arms.

*The past several years have been spent clinging desperately to His promises as He has stretched me into someone I hardly recognize.* He is faithfully nurturing this widow and transforming me on the inside just as drastically as my life has changed on the outside.

Truthfully, I mess up often and sometimes in big ways; but I am learning to live life by the Spirit one tiny, baby step at a time. By continually tapping into the power of the Holy One dwelling inside of me, I find access to the fruit of His Spirit. I have a long way to go in my transformation, but the glimpses of where His power is slowly taking me; well they look something like this:

*More ***loving*** and empathetic towards others.

\****Joyful***, even in my deepest of sorrow.

\****Peaceful*** inside in the midst of a life that looks to be in chaotic change from the outside.

*A tiny bit more ***patient*** (personally not my strongest attribute).

*Softer and ***kinder***, both to others and to myself (which is huge for this rehabilitating perfectionist).

*Choosing ***good*** things…good attitudes, good words, good facial expressions, and good actions.

\****Faithfully*** believing He has control of my life and the lives of my loved ones.

*A ***gentleness*** that doesn't distract from strength but instead enhances it.

*Calm ***self-control***, focused more on obedience to my Savior and less on me controlling anything.

This transforming of every part of me, it hurts sometimes. I think of it as earning my "Spiritual stretch marks". The stretching is not pleasant, but the reward is phenomenal! Spiritual stretch marks reflect the growth God is creating in my heart and I am grateful that He redeems my pain to use for His glory.

Can you relate? Have you noticed a softening of your spirit as you nestle deeper into the arms of our

Father during this all-changing whirlwind of widowhood? Sisters, as one who is walking this road too, I gently urge you to tap into the transforming power of the Holy Spirit. Tap in and then watch how God stretches you while growing His fruits within you.

*Father God, You are faithful to produce spiritual fruit in my life when I hand over control to You. Thank You for the work You are doing in my heart, as You transform me more into Your likeness. There is such beauty in the woman You desire for me to be. You are patient as You mold me and stretch me, You are forgiving when I forget to surrender, and You are gracious and kind. Lord, help me keep in step with Your Spirit within me. Amen.*

**March 19**

**There are No Do-Overs**

By Sherry Rickard

I have a secret to tell...I am selfish, controlling, and I'm not always happy. Phew! I got that out! Now, for an explanation...

*But the tongue can no man tame; it is an unruly evil, full of deadly poison. Therewith bless we God, even the Father; and therewith curse we men, which are made after the likeness of God. Out of the same mouth proceedeth blessing and cursing. My brethren, these things ought not so to be- James 3:8-10 KJV*

I am almost four years into this grief journey, and as I type this article I am preparing for this ministry's upcoming conference.

As I march into the days and hours leading up to the conference, I have been bombarded with flashbacks of terrible moments at the end of my husband's life; the moments where I did not use my tongue to God's glory. Those are moments I wish I could erase. The things I said and decisions I made were made in my flesh, thinking I had more time.

One flashback includes choosing not to stay the night in the transplant wing, even when my husband asked. I had been at the hospital since before breakfast, and I was very tired. I told him I needed to go home, so I could re-fuel and come back to love on him the next day. I thought we'd have "tomorrow". I never slept with my husband again; nor did I ever wake up near him again.

Another flashback was the last conversation I had with my husband in the ICU. Bill's friends were visiting us, and they had travelled a long distance to visit him. Bill wanted just me and kept saying to me, "I

42

love you; I love you; I love you" and holding tightly to my hands and pulling me close and kissing me - over and over again. I felt the pull of his friends wanting time with him, and I told him I would see him soon. I gave my time with Bill to them...I would never have another conversation with him again.

Do not take the present moment for granted. Love like you don't have tomorrow. Forgive as though your life depends on it. Share as though you are the only resource available. Speak with love. Once the moment is over, you will regret it if you didn't handle it with grace and love. **There are no do-overs**. Satan uses these moments to attack me and stunt my grief journey. I have to call on my sisters and brothers in Christ to carry me when I am attacked with these moments.

God is good and He sustains me, through the Holy Spirit who strengthens and comforts me. Prayer supports me. I can, through Christ, move past these memories and into the Truth. Bill knows I loved him and knows that in both of those moments; I made the correct choice with the information I had at the time. That thought helps to remind me that I need to be busy about the Lord's work here. If I sit and think on these moments I could have handled better, I am looking back and not moving forward. If I am busy about the Lord's work, then I am moving forward and thinking about my Savior; not regrets, memories, and what ifs.

*Sweet Father, Thank You for reminding me to look to You when the memories of what-ifs come to mind. Thank You for Your grace and mercy and for Your Word which sustains me. Thank You for my brothers and sisters in Christ who continue to point me to You. I love You, Lord! In Jesus name, Amen*

## March 20

## The Table Was Set

By Linda Lint

*You prepare a table before me in the presence of my enemies.*
*Psalm 23:5 NIV*

That Thursday morning dawned grey and bleak, matching my mood. Only seven months into widowhood, I was facing my first Thanksgiving without my beloved.

I had insisted my daughter spend the day out of town with friends because I knew I would most likely not be very good company. She only agreed to go after I promised her I would attend a gathering at a local church with some friends.

As the morning progressed, I kept thinking of excuses to gracefully bow out. My mind was filled with memories of past holiday celebrations and I missed my husband terribly. I could not imagine how I would get through the day without breaking down. There would be no turkey, no fine dishes, no special appetizer tray and - no husband.

However, I remembered my promise to my daughter and knew she would be terribly upset if she found out I had spent the day alone. So, I made my way to the church and as soon as I entered the door the enemies of loneliness and sorrow started screaming at me. I wanted to turn around and run! But God had a different plan! Before I could make a quick exit, my friend appeared, got me settled in and ushered me to the appetizer table.

I could not believe what I saw before me!
Seeing my shock, my friend was very concerned, until
I explained to her that this was exactly the same type
of foods I had made for my family for so many holiday
meals - exactly the same - cheeses, pickles, olives, meat,
crackers - even the dip. Now, there is no possible way
the person who prepared this array could have known
my family history - but God did! When I was able to
talk to the dear lady who had prepared these treats, she
told me she just felt "led" to do it this way this year "for
some reason".

After a pleasant time of fellowship and
enjoying a sampling of it all, I found myself ready to
break down and made a hasty retreat to the ladies
room. Thankfully, I was alone and, after composing
myself, my intention was to once again find a way to
leave. But, once again, God had another plan! As soon
as I returned to the gathering, my friend was waiting
for me and ushered me to a table for the meal.

Once again, I was met with a surprise. There
before me was a table set with some of the most
beautiful dishes I have ever seen - a full set of red
depression glass - complete with candlesticks. I felt like
royalty. This was so different from the paper plate
dinner at the care center the year before.

And, what a meal it was! Would it surprise you
when I say the meal included all of the foods I was
accustomed to having? Everything was the same - even
to the detail of the jellied cranberry sauce (my personal
favorite).

It came time to leave and, on the drive home,
as I was thanking God for His love and care, He sent
me this message -" Beloved today I prepared a table for
you in the presence of your enemies". And yes He did

- for my enemies that day were taunting me - the enemies of grief, loneliness and fear of the future - I sat and I ate at the table God Himself (with the help of many servants) provided for me.

I will rest easy knowing that He has only good things for me - holidays and every day yet to come.

*Dear Father, sometimes loneliness and sorrow clouds my vision of You in my life. I know You are there and always with me. I thank You for Your loving care and provision. Amen*

## March 21

## It's Just a Long Way Home

By Nancy Howell

I. miss. my. husband.

There, I said it. It stinks to be a widow around any of the holidays

Last year, at this time, with the gaping wound of the loss of my husband still fresh, I walked through the stores (and life) in a bit of a trance, much like a survivor in a war zone.

But I still miss him this year. He was a force of nature, a "man's man", a 6'3" lanky handsome dude. He was an outdoorsman, a wonderful provider, a Godly man who was the best, most patient, hands-on daddy I had ever witnessed first-hand.

I ache for that physical presence, his strong hand linked in mine. My boys miss the almost-nightly wrestling matches, held in our den, where giggling and laughter filled our home.

I've learned how to get along without him. But it hasn't been easy. I have to keep reminding myself that we all are on a journey--I like to call mine "unimagined"--and that everyone has trials, heartaches, and folks they miss physically in their lives. I have to keep myself immersed in God's Word and in His music.

I found out the hard way a few weeks back that I cannot venture too far ahead of God in this journey, nor let go of His hand. "Self" got in the way, I was feeling pretty good, and I depended on **me** and **me alone**. Let's just say I tripped and skinned my knee spiritually.

Like a small child, I cried, ran to my Heavenly Daddy, crawled back up in His lap, and was instantly soothed. I learned my lesson, at least this time. I won't walk too far ahead again, and will keep within an arm's length of God, so I can quickly grasp onto His hand if needed.

As Isaiah so beautifully writes:
*Can a mother forget the infant at her breast,*
*walk away from the baby she bore?*
*But even if mothers forget,*
*I'd never forget you--NEVER.*
*Look, I've written your names on the backs of my*
hands.
*Isaiah 49:15-16 (the Message)*

God won't forget us. He can't, He has our names written/carved/emblazoned/tattooed on the backs of His hands!

And in this journey, this unimagined-unspeakable-sometimes-seemingly-unbearable-life that we each have been blessed with, God will give us the endurance we need to keep walking the path.

*Heavenly Father, I ask for wisdom and strength for my journey. Help me see the good, even when the bad seems to be overwhelming. You and You alone have the means to turn the bad into something beautiful. Let me never walk too far ahead without Your hand in mine. Keep reminding me of my purpose this side of Heaven. In Jesus' name, Amen.*

## March 22

## Palm Sunday

By Danita Hiles

I had a great post all written for this morning. Then Palm Sunday happened.

It was one of those sermons where everyone else could have stayed home- this one was just for me!

It's been a rough two weeks at my house. Mean girls and standardized testing both chipped away at my girls' self-confidence. Crumbling stucco showed evidence of my house's need of repair. I made a HUGE financial mistake –which will cost me time and money to rectify. My precious sister continues to struggle in her fight against a debilitating disease. And so on....

Then I heard these words on Sunday morning:

*As Jesus rode into Jerusalem on Palm Sunday, throngs of people crowded around, waving palm branches, singing praises, straining for a glimpse of the King. The One who would end it all. The One who was promised to save them. 'Hosanna, Hosanna', they cried. 'Blessed is He who comes in the name of the Lord.' One week later, those same crowds cried out again. 'Crucify Him, Crucify Him', they cried. 'Give us Barabbas instead.'*

One week. Seven days.

What had happened in one week to change their cry from praise to accusation?

To cause them to put down their palm branches of praise and to raise clenched fists in the air?

Simply this. **Things were not working out the way they thought they should.**

They imagined a King riding in victory to change it all. Prosperity. Victory. Freedom.

Instead, they got a humble servant, carrying a Cross- walking to His death. Followed by taunts and jeers. Sentenced to die.

Where is the victory in that?

I can relate.

Somehow in the back of my mind is the thought that since we have lost so much, since my girls have lost their dad and grandparents, since I have had to walk the path of widowhood, things should be a little easier. The way should be smoother.

Sometimes I get mad because things are not working out the way I think they should.

And in those times, I can easily switch from a heart of praise and thankfulness and trust, to a heart of disappointment and dismay. How quickly my cry can shift from adoration to accusation. *Why, Lord, why'? 'How can You let this happen?' 'Where is there any victory in this ugly'?*

*Precious Jesus – as I walk through this Easter week, forgive me for my doubt. Forgive me for my lack of trust. Forgive me for joining the crowd and raising my fist in the air in accusation against the ugliness of life. I choose to trust You. No matter what. Thank You for Your faithfulness. You were willing to die. For me. You have promised to work all things together for good. Even when things are not working out that way I think they should. You are the King of Kings and Lord of Lords. And Your kingdom is forever.*

## March 23

## Cloudy Days

By Julie Wright

The rainy season is upon us here in South Florida. Our afternoons are filled with large, billowing, and dark clouds charging in from the west like mighty giants who unleash torments of rain that darken the afternoon sky to the point where it looks like nighttime. The days meld together like one continuous storm that seems to have no end. The forecast feels gloomy and sad and we long for brighter, sunnier days to appear again for us.

The widowhood journey can sometimes feel that way too. A close family friend of ours lost her husband just a few weeks ago. He went in for routine surgery and never made it home. We shook our heads and wondered why such a tragedy could happen and then the clouds begin to roll in...

The clouds of sorrow, distress, isolation, and loneliness. The clouds surge in quickly and fill our minds with an overcast forecast of our new futures. They cause a haze that doesn't allow us to see clearly, if at all. The clouds cause us to feel drained, empty and exhausted; but mostly alone. We wonder when they will stop and if the sun will peer out again, if even just for a moment.

As I sat on my patio this afternoon watching the clouds roll in again, I prayed for my friend. My heart began to ache for her knowing the journey was far from over and that more cloudy days would be ahead for her. In fact, just talking with her and remembering cloudy days along my own journey made a new cloud roll into my heart and life. It's strange how this widowhood path can fill up with cloudy days in the blink of an eye.

The storm clouds passed through our neighborhood quickly today with a brief but strong shower of rain. Thankfully, just as quickly the sunlight was shining again, glistening on the dewdrops left behind on our flowers.

I smiled as I realized that while the clouds seem dark, heavy and intimidating at times, the sun never stops shining above them. We may not be able to see the sun all the time, but it's there. He's there…in His full glory, brilliance and beauty. He watches the clouds billow and rage over us, sometimes to the point where all we see is darkness; we can't see Him, but He sees us.

I picked up my Bible and began looking at verses relating to clouds. I found verse after verse that told of God's glory and care being in those clouds.

If the clouds of widowhood are surrounding you today and all you see are endless storms of isolation, pain, sorrow and emptiness, please remember that the sun is still shining behind those clouds. That God is right there with you. **Whether or not you can see or feel his presence; He is there**. Ready to shine down on you with hope, tranquility, joy, and peace. Let the clouds surge and swell around you. Let the rains of your sadness and loneliness flow from them and then look up and **see the Son again**…He'll be there. He promises.

*Heavenly Father, help me look past the haze and mist caused from the storms and clouds that fill our lives along this tough and fragile widowhood journey, to find the beauty, brilliance and love in You and Your Word. Although I sometimes lose sight of You from the overcast and isolating clouds of fear, doubt and grief; deep down, I know You are there. I will look to the heavens with great hope and expectation for storms or sunshine, knowing You are in both. Amen.*


## March 24

### What's Your Boaz's Field?

By Kit Hinkle

What's your "Boaz's field"?

Maybe you aren't sure who Boaz is. In case you're not familiar with Ruth, she is the widow in the Old Testament and the picture of obedience. The Lord rewarded her obedience by having His hand in what she thought was a random selection over which field to glean. God placed her in Boaz's field. Boaz's family relation to Ruth's mother-in-law set the stage for a future so big, Ruth would never have conceived it on her own.

Does the Lord already have me right now in my "Boaz's field"?

When I study the story of Ruth, I notice how, at some point, Ruth's obedience moved from immediate actions which served the needs of the day (gleaning the fields) to more proactive steps to affect her future.

Under the guidance of her mother-in-law, Ruth waited until all the field hands were sleeping to slip under the blanket at the feet of Boaz as he slept . When Boaz noticed her there, he was taken by her appeal for him to marry her. Being a relative of Ruth's mother-in-law, Boaz could redeem Naomi's land and restore their social position by marrying Ruth.

Think about what a risk Ruth took there. A woman sleeping at the feet of a man? Clearly a bold move like that isn't something the Lord would normally encourage you to do!

This direction to Ruth wasn't given out of the blue. When Ruth received those instructions, she had been walking in trust and obedience for a long time. First she was obedient and loyal in coming to this land with Naomi rather than going back to her own land. Then gleaning the fields. Imagine how in-tune Ruth must have been to true versus false directions—enough to be able to discern that sleeping at a man's feet was, in fact, something the Lord approved of her doing.

If I have been truly faithful, truly obedient to what the Lord has called me to do, eventually He will reveal a plan to me for my future. Has He already? What "Boaz's field" has God placed me in which will springboard me into the future? What does God want me to do about it? **I will recognize it only if I've been walking in obedience.** Am I listening, and am I bold enough to execute it?

*Father God, I pray that You grow our hearts to be optimistic and open like Ruth's, and reveal to each of us what "Boaz's fields" you have placed in our lives. In the name of your precious Son, I pray for softening and changes upon all of us. Amen.*

## March 25

## Choosing to Remain Single

By Lori Reynolds Streller

"You are young, *you will remarry.*"

"You still have a lot of life left ahead of you, *you will remarry.*"

"You and the kids are awesome, *you will remarry.*"

Honestly, hearing these comments makes me cringe. I was married for nineteen years; I know firsthand that marriage is a wonderful thing. I was loved well. We made a great team.

At forty-three, I am (God willing) merely half way through my life expectancy. And yes, we have a pretty awesome family; we love to laugh and we have fun.

**Guess what?** I am content. I am not interested in marrying again.

Each time I say this, I get the {smile and nod} and a comment similar to "Well, it's early; you are still heavy in grief."

I am going to make a bold statement here so listen carefully.

**There is a difference in being content with where God has you and just getting stuck here; settling into a "victim mode" of "nothing will ever be as good as it was".**

I am not clinging to a false remembrance of marital perfection. Marriage is hard work. It is a daily sacrifice of choosing to place the marital relationship as the most important earthly bond. Life wants to get in the way and we have to be intentional in our loving of each other to build a strong, godly marriage. I am not choosing to remain single because I am "glamorizing" my marriage into something it wasn't.

I am contentedly living the life my Savior has allowed me to live.

**I am accepting the "right here" and the "right now" and living fully in it.**

Here's the deal, ladies. The Bible is clear on this topic. Our marriage covenant ends upon the death of our spouse. Widows <u>can</u> remarry. It's just that I don't _personally_ have any desire to share this life with a man other than my late husband. None. And whether friends and acquaintances are okay with this decision or not, doesn't really concern me.

**What I WANT is to be so aligned with God's will for my life that I am able to accept His plans for my future, whether they are what I currently desire or not.**

Maybe friends are correct and God will have another beautiful marriage relationship in my future. Maybe He won't. I am truly okay either way, but honestly, _in this moment_, it is not my heart's desire.

So here is what I am feeling led to pray:

_Lord, you know my heart. You placed in it a deep love for my husband and you blessed us with a beautiful marriage. To be loved by Tim for our 19 years was enough for me. Thank you for surrounding me with friends in my life who have good intentions and are concerned for my future. I am trusting that if You have plans for another marriage covenant in my life, You will change my heart, until then, I am content with where You have me._

If I've learned nothing else on this journey, I've learned these two things:

**Life doesn't always go as planned, and God is faithful.**

He is faithful and I trust him to take me where I need to go, when I need to be there.

So when others feel the need to "encourage me" with the statement that I will marry again, I have a choice. I can dig my heels in and argue, or I can let their words softly open a new place within me.

My initial response of defensive thoughts are slowly transforming into a perspective that has <u>much less</u> to do with remarrying and <u>much more</u> to do with the condition of my heart.

*"I will instruct you and teach you in the way you should go; I will counsel you and watch over you." ~Psalm 32:8 NIV*

## March 26

## The Tunnel

By Linda Lint

> *Commit your way to the Lord - trust in Him.*
> *Psalm 37:5 NIV*

Twenty years later, I can still remember the darkness of that tunnel.

We were on a train, traveling to the Midwest from California - on our way to a new home and a new life. Neither my husband nor I enjoyed flying and we definitely were not enthusiastic about driving some three thousand miles with two children! So, the train was a logical choice.

The trip was going well - beautiful scenery in Colorado and a pretty smooth ride - until I heard about "the tunnel". The time had come in our journey when the train was no longer able to take "the long way around" the mountain - in order to get to the other side of the high Rockies it had to go through a tunnel.

We were prepared early in the day and told of the necessity for lights off to preserve power; a slower pace for safety and our need to relax, stay in our seats, and trust the engineer who knew what he was doing.

The ride through this tunnel took several minutes and it was so incredibly dark that I could not see my own hand in front of my face! No lights, no sound - just the darkness and the steady, sure, constant movement forward of the train - AND the comforting presence of my husband next to me.

Honestly, I did not enjoy that particular part of the trip, and I would have avoided it if there had been some other way. However, I knew if we were to get where we were going, we had to go through that tunnel.

Sounds a lot like this journey we are on, doesn't it, dear sisters? We are on a train of sorrow traveling through the tunnel of grief. Some of us are just entering the tunnel, some are part way through and some are beginning to get closer to the light at the end. This is not a part of the journey through life that any of us wanted - but we know in order to get where we are going this tunnel is necessary. It is difficult to relax and let the "train" move forward. Because this time we don't have our beloved spouses by our side, and the darkness is so overwhelming.

We must take comfort in knowing that this particular train is not guided by a human engineer. This train is guided by God Himself - He is not only the engineer - He is also sitting next to us - right there alongside.

Corrie Ten Boom said this: "When a train goes through a tunnel, and it gets dark, you don't throw away the ticket and jump off - You sit still and trust the engineer."

I wanted to get off that train then and so many times during the last three years I have wanted to "get off". But, I realize I have no choice - for if I am to see the light again and get where I am going, I must relax and let my loving God be the engineer.

And, by the way, when I got through that tunnel into the light again I was rewarded with some of the most breathtaking scenery I have ever experienced. The trip through the tunnel was hard; but, the reward was worth it.

*Dear Father, Trusting You when there is light is difficult. Trusting You when there is darkness and uncertainty is overwhelming. I want to pace and fret and rush through the journey - I want to get to the light again. Look upon me, Father, and give me an image of You as the Engineer of this particular journey. Amen*

## March 27

### Peace Over the Past

By Kit Hinkle

*Indeed, I count everything as loss because of the surpassing worth of knowing Christ Jesus my Lord.*

*Philippians 3:8 ESV*

Several times in the past week I've heard single women describe their sense of feeling lost or weary from this journey of going it alone without their companion.

"It's not just that I miss *having* a husband," Kara, a young single mom, shared. "I miss *him*."

"I've thrown myself into service hoping to see fruit from my work; I'm tired. I work every day without my husband to give me companionship," Julie said. She and her husband didn't have kids, and together they enjoyed careers and ministry. She now finds it hard to carry the joy of that labor by herself.

Do you relate to these women's suffering?

If so, Sister, don't accept this as permanent. Feeling lost is a normal reaction to the initial shock of grief. Sometimes it's necessary to process these feelings while a burden simply sits on us. Scripture gives us help on how to make it through this "wilderness".

### *Identify with Christ's Suffering*

In Philippians 3:10, Paul says, *"That I may know him and the power of his resurrection, and may share his sufferings, becoming like him in his death."* Think about the man who is saying this and all that he suffered. In his ministry he was beaten, stoned, whipped, ridiculed, put in prison, and shipwrecked. He endured these things as a way to share in Christ's sufferings and be more like Christ.

We can imitate Christ when we choose to be patient with our friends who say the wrong thing during our grieving. We die to ourselves when we stick to our responsibilities rather than run from them to tend to our own wounds. Enduring loneliness this way allows us to identify with Christ's suffering.

### *Identify with Christ's Resurrection*

Philippians 3:11 explains something Christ has done that we can't physically do until the end of our life—be physically resurrected from the dead. Paul says, *"That by any means possible I may attain the resurrection from the dead."*

We can't achieve that now, but don't you think we are being resurrected out of our grief each day as we grow in our relationship to Christ? As we set our heart and mind on Him, this feeling of being lost won't last forever. We can look forward to healing and clarity in our lives.

### *Press On*

In Philippians 3:12, Paul explains how through these struggles he presses on. *"Not that I have already obtained this or am already perfect, but I press on to make it my own, because Christ Jesus has made me his own."* Sister, know that this season of obedience during a lonely time is part of His plan. Don't be afraid of it. You are being sculpted into a beautiful creation, one that can serve His purpose for His kingdom.

That may not feel great to hear when you're yearning for more. You may want to feel the loving arms of the husband you lost. You may want the goals you've set for moving forward achieved faster than they seem to be taking.

But have grace with yourself. Start to pull yourself out of the "wilderness" by remembering that even Paul himself, the great evangelist who changed the course of history, identified with Christ's suffering. He too looked forward to being resurrected and whole. But he kept his eye on the prize, Jesus: his Companion in the wilderness.

Everyone goes through this. There is hope, and you're not alone.

*Lord Jesus, please put Your loving arms around me and encourage me that I will not suffer with these burdens forever. Help me come to You and be courageous to cry out to You with questions. Then give me hope from Your Word that I can trust You with my future. Give me peace over the past, so I can know I will not always be in this wilderness. Amen.*

# March 28

## Great Plans

By Sherry Rickard

*For I know the thoughts that I think toward you, saith the Lord, thoughts of peace, and not of evil, to give you an expected end.*

*Jeremiah 29:11 KJV*

A few months ago, God washed the intention of this familiar verse over me anew.

Practically all of my adult life, my road has been the "hard road". My first marriage ended and, with a three year old to care for, I became a single mom. After five years I was introduced to my second husband, Bill. We were married and, for six months, were blissfully in love. Bill got sick and for the next four years, I learned about sacrificial love. God allowed me the honor of loving Bill as he walked Home. I was a single mom again, and it was so hard! I had counted on growing old with Bill; making a ton of memories and growing our testimonies together. It was very hard to accept that God did not have the same plans that we did...that I did. It took me some time to work on my heart. I had to allow God to minister to me and show me that His plans are always good.

As I walked out of the dark shadows of grief, I realized my need to lean on Christ. So, I forced myself to read the Scriptures, combing them for promises and clinging to those. I wrote down references so I could refer to them often. Of course, Jeremiah 29:11 was at the top of the list.

I would tell myself in my deepest moments of grief that the Lord has thoughts of peace toward me, to give me (Sherry) an expected end. Peace wasn't what I was feeling; but I continued to cling to that promise.

In recent weeks, I have begun to see what the Lord has planned for me at this point in my journey- **thoughts of peace**. He has allowed me to grieve and lean on Him, as He prepared a blessing for me designed to meet my needs where I am on the road right now. It brings me peace. It brings me closer to Him.

Had I not travelled this road - allowing time for stopping along the way and sitting down to deal with the vantage point at that spot in the road and then standing up and walking a little further - I would have missed all of the healing that I have been honored to have. I have met fellow travelers along the way who have strengthened me, sharpened me, imparted wisdom to me and held me. I am better for having travelled this road. I have peace. The Lord has given me a new mission and my heart bursts at the honor of being entrusted with another job assignment from God Almighty.

So, my dear sisters, wherever you are on this road, please know that the Lord has thoughts of peace toward you. If you are walking or sitting; be open to His calling and know He has great plans for you.

It is only when I lean back into His arms that I realize the blessings are coming, and then the peace comes.

Stay on this road, sweet sisters. Take time and stop to rest when you need to, but continue the journey. **God has great plans for you and they include peace.**

*Dear Lord, Thank You for Your promises in Scripture. Thank You for loving me. Thank You for peace. Amen*

## March 29

## Amazing Love

By Lori Reynolds Streller

*He was delivered over to death for our sins*
*and was raised to life for our justification.*

Romans 4:25 NIV

I sit in a doctor's waiting room again today; walking the cold, sterile halls to an exam room; discussing symptoms and pain issues with a specialist. This time I am with my daughter instead of my husband, but the memories flood me just the same.

No, she doesn't have cancer. No, her condition isn't life threatening. But the hours spent with her through an exam and then in the lab for massive blood draws were all too familiar to me.

She has some type of auto immune disease, one that is hard to pinpoint and diagnose; a chronic illness that doesn't present with typical symptoms. The fact that her disease is unknown doesn't eliminate the reality of her joint pain. It doesn't dismiss that she has sat out of Cross Country and Softball seasons because it hurts too much to do the things she enjoys.

I don't like seeing my daughter suffer.

No parent likes to see their child suffering.

Ahhhhh, and with that thought, the light bulb blinks on in my heart.

*NO PARENT*...

**God the Father** did not enjoy seeing **His** Son suffering.

In Matthew 26:38-39, Jesus Christ was overwhelmed with sorrow. He asked for God to take the cup of suffering from Him.

Can you even imagine? The all-powerful God, who *could* end the suffering of His Son, chose not to. I cannot comprehend the restraint that must have taken. What intense heartache.

Jesus finishes His request with these nine words, "Yet not as I will, but as you will."

Oh, how the Father must have been beaming with pride over his Son's submission; *a total submission that led all the way to the cross.*

Christ asked again in verse forty-two, "My Father, if it is not possible for this cup to be taken away unless I drink it, may your will be done." And again, in verse forty-four, Jesus makes His same request.

This repeated plea for help, coupled with unwavering willingness to obey, shakes me to my core.

I want to stop the pain my daughter experiences on a daily basis. I cannot.

God's love for us is so unfathomably great, that He allowed His Son to suffer, knowing it was the only way for us to spend eternity with Him. Even knowing that Christ would be victorious over death, God's heart must have grieved at His suffering. Jesus' cup of suffering was the separation from God that would occur when He took on the sins of the world. He faced a double death. I imagine that spiritual separation was even more painful than the physical death for Christ.

Jesus, being God Himself, was given the power to lay down His life. (John 10:17-18) He, as the Son of God, always obeys the will of His Father. He stayed on the cross. He stayed to become our way of salvation.

God didn't stop His suffering.

He is God the *Father*. He knows what it is like to watch a child suffer and yet His love for us is so vast that He permitted it.

I wouldn't choose for my child to suffer in order for me to have a relationship with you, Sister. I certainly wouldn't expect you to sacrifice your child in order to know me. Yet that's exactly what God did for each of us.

**He**

**amazes**

**me.**

*Thank You, Lord, that You are a loving God. Your love for me transcends my knowledge. I cannot wrap my brain around the depth of Your love for mankind that You would sacrifice Your Son for my redemption, but I am so grateful that You did. You amaze me, Lord. Amen.*

## March 30

## The Hope We Have!

By Erika Graham

> *And so, Lord, where do I put my hope?*
> *My only hope is in YOU.*
> Psalm 39:7 NLV

Do you ever wonder why we all sound so hopeful? How we have such faith? Why we can write such meaningful things?

Well, sisters, it's not **us** at all, but it's **Christ** in us. It comes out of our obedience to His leading and humbling ourselves before Him, trusting His plan for us.

Let us share....

Easter is the day all Christians no matter their denomination stand united saying, "He is Risen, He is Risen, Indeed."

What does that mean?

God sent His Son Jesus to earth. He was fully God and fully man. He walked this earth and was tempted. He saw suffering. He saw hurt. He saw pain. He rejoiced and celebrated. He had friends. He had loved ones. He experienced and witnessed every human emotion and trial.

Except He was without sin!

Then He made the ultimate sacrifice... He humbly took on death and the consequences of sin at the cross.

He did this willingly!

Through His death, burial, and resurrection He paid the price once and for all for each of us.

The Bible is clear, if we believe with our whole heart and confess it with our mouths, we are immediately forgiven and we are saved, our name is then sealed in the book of life. (Romans 10:9 and John 14:6)

As Christian widows, we speak of hope and faith because we know that Christ died on that cross for *us*. We've professed our faith in His sacrifice. We've invited Him into our hearts and lives. We've vowed to not live perfect, happy lives on our *own* strength, but to live imperfectly, messy lives in *Christ Jesus*.

**It's not about religion, sisters, but it is about a personal relationship with Jesus**.

We know the hope we have comes from God. We grieve not in a hopeless manner unsure of where our husbands are, or where we will end up. We are not vessels floating around in a sea, just haphazardly swaying here and there. We have Christ at the helm of our lives, and we know for certain because of our faith, we will stand in glory someday before God, and we will be reunited with our beloved husbands.

That's called "hopeful grief"!

We'd like to ask you...

Do you have this same hope?

Are you standing with us today arm in arm professing the same faith?

Do you have Christ in your heart?

If not, or you're unsure, then this is what you can do. Pray, sisters. Invite God in. Profess your faith in Christ's sacrifice at the cross. Accept the free gift of salvation.

If you're not sure how to do that then pray this prayer:

*Father God, I believe that you sent Jesus to this earth, and that He was the true son of God. I believe that Jesus did die on the cross for my sins, but then rose again victoriously. I ask that you come into my heart and mind and that you reveal all your truths to me. Lord I commit my life to you, and I choose to live a life that will please you. Lord I ask for your forgiveness for my sins. I pray that as I move forward now that my eyes will be opened to all you want to teach me. In your precious matchless name, Amen*

Sisters, if you just asked Christ into your heart the Bible says there is rejoicing in Heaven (Luke 15:7). How amazing!

Please let us know (through the website www.anewseason.net) that you have made this decision and have chosen to walk in faith. We would love to talk with you and pray for you. We hope each of you have a peaceful and blessed Resurrection Day. He is Risen, He is Risen Indeed!!

## March 31

## HE is the Spring!

By Ami Atkins

For this southern girl, winter in northern Illinois is especially brutal. Snow is endless. The wind is a torrent of frigid blasts that chills to the very core. The trees are barren and naked, all signs of life snatched from them. For months the world exists only in shades of black and white. The sky is diluted, a watercolor with too much water and not enough paint. The sun is forever hidden behind a wall of impenetrable gray. Sorrow, discouragement, and despair run rampant, magnified by the bleakness of the weather outside. I have learned what it is to long for spring.

Eagerly I awaited the return of birds, and green, and sun, and warmth. Just when it seemed we were to be forever enslaved by the White Witch, a robin flitted across the sky! A daffodil pushed its way upward, blooming defiantly in the face of snow. Spring! It does exist! The landscape here has yet to fully explode in its array of colors, but it is coming. As sure as the sun rises and sets, so will dormant trees produce the fresh green of budding leaves.

In winter the earth lay silent, waiting, clinging to the figment of green hidden deep beneath the snow. In winter my soul lay silent, waiting, clinging to the hope that life and love and beauty would come again. But I'm caught between winter and spring, I think.

One word the Holy Spirit impresses. Wait. So I wait with bated breath. The branch is not dead, just pruned severely. Tentatively, new growth begins to blossom. I wait. I believe the colors will be vibrant and the fruit lush. Eagerly I await. What's next God? Perhaps there will be spring. "Produce what is most beautiful to you, Lord."

Winter, in due time, will come again. Yet I am not afraid. Without winter, there would be no spring. Without death, there is no resurrection. It's winter that taught me my desperate need.

I have learned what it is to long for Jesus.

And so, also on that fateful Saturday between the cross and the resurrection, all creation lay silent, waiting, holding its collective breath. Had the powers of hell prevailed? Would He rise again as He said? The dark of night is greatest just before the dawn. All hope was lost. The Savior was dead, apparently not really the Savior at all.

But wait. As Sunday crept over the horizon, light eradicated darkness. Life burst forth from barren trees! Colors spread through a world painted gray! And all creation shouted, *"Death is swallowed up in victory. O death where us your victory? O death where is your sting?"* (I Corinthians 15:54-55 ESV)

The spark catches, so I join the triumph song. "Up from the grave He arose, with a might triumph o'er His foes!" As the new life of spring erupts from the death of winter, so did Jesus rise. He arose the Victor.

*Lord Jesus, You are victorious. You have won. And one day even physical death will be defeated. You are hope. You are life. You are Spring. Amen.*

# APRIL

## April 1

### All Things New

By Kit Hinkle

*Therefore, if anyone is in Christ, he is a new creation. The old
has passed away; behold, the new has come.*
*2 Corinthians 5:17 NIV*

"I make all things new."

I pondered those words as I looked at a huge, rugged woodened-beam cross mounted from the ceiling at my church.

I remembered earlier in my walk as a widow, missing my husband so badly. He was ripped away so suddenly, I had no choice but to move forward. I had a slew of kids to raise, siblings and a mother who needed my attention. At first I plowed forward, hoping to skip over the mountain of grief one can't avoid.

But, oh, how impossible it was to deny my sadness. That marriage was good. Life had been joyous. The memory of it all pulled me back— had me stop in my tracks many times and just be, well, sad. Sad enough to wonder, am I stuck?

I thought about how it was when I first met my husband—all things were new—I was younger, no kids yet except my two future step children and they were new too—all new. Exciting. New.

"I make all things new," Jesus says, and He's right. These things that I kept in my heart were things I can remember and take time to grieve, and then surrender, letting Him make all things new—All new love for each and every person in my life--those who have been there forever, and those who come in new to my life.

That huge, rugged cross represents all things new. I continued to stare at it until my heart melted. He has truly come to fill my heart completely. He makes all things new!

I can start all over again. I can consider all things new—shed the old skin and grieve fully enough so that I can look at my life like I did when I had those eyes of youth, fresh with wonder of what the future might hold!

*Dear Heavenly Father, help me see my future is all new. As long as I have breath in me, I can build again, love again and impact others for eternity! Amen*

**Happy Easter, precious Sisters. Use His saving resurrection to begin all things new today.**

## April 2

## Right Where I Am Meant To Be

By Karen Emberlin

> *The Lord will work out his plans for my life,*
> *for your faithful love, O Lord, endures forever.*
> *Psalm 138:8 NLT*

There are many times I do not understand why God has put me in certain places or brought circumstances into my life. However, when I look back, it begins to make sense, and I realize I was "right where I was meant to be".

My husband was not ill, so we had no idea God was preparing to take him "home". Our daily routines seemed to be quite normal. I can vividly remember the work projects we were doing, church activities we were involved in, places we ate, and even a few out-of-the-ordinary activities for us. Birthdays were not a big thing with us, but my husband decided we would take the day off on my last birthday with him to enjoy lunch at a favorite restaurant, go to an afternoon movie, and shop at my favorite store. It was such a fun day and I sure hoped he would suggest it again!

As certain holidays approached, it became evident that it was not going to be possible to spend time with our family. In the forty-eight years we were married, this had only happened one other time. I was so disappointed. However, I remember telling a friend at church, even though my husband and I would be spending the holidays without family, I was very thankful that we would be together as we had two families from our home town that had just lost their spouses.

We attended the service at church and then enjoyed a quiet day. We connected with our children and grandchildren through Skype, and went to a new convenience store near our home for a hot dog – but we were together!!

As I look back over those last weeks we had together, I now realize God had us (me) "right where He meant us to be". He was giving us some very special time together, and we did not even know it! We were able to enjoy holidays, and our forty-eighth wedding anniversary – *one last time* - as my husband made his unexpected journey "home" a few days later.

Yes, holidays are bittersweet for me, but I thank God for the precious years my husband and I were able to share them, and for the memories we created together. My life is not the same without him, and no one will ever take his place!

However, I am so thankful God loves me (even more than my husband did) and He has a specific place for me. I may not always know exactly where this specific place is, but I know He does!

*For I know the plans I have for you, says the Lord. They are plans for good and not for evil, to give you a future and a hope. In those days when you pray, I will listen. You will find me when you seek me, if you look for me in earnest.*

*Jeremiah 29:11-13 (TLB)*

*Lord, help me to seek You in earnest and trust You daily to guide me to the place where You want me to be. Amen*

## April 3

## My Own Empty Tomb

By Leah Stirewalt

As the anniversary of my husband's suicide rapidly nears, I've been doing a lot of pondering. Easter was our last holiday together, and as we celebrate Easter again, I face many bittersweet emotions.

As I pondered Christ's empty tomb that we, who are His followers, so gloriously celebrate, I realized that I, too, have an empty tomb to celebrate. My tomb? Grief.

I've lived in a "grief tomb" off and on this past year. I have, at times, felt literally buried in my grief...suffocating on occasion...no air from the outside. But the day came when the "stone" to my "grief tomb" was rolled away, and I walked out. I could see light again at the end of a very dark tunnel. I caught a glimpse of some of the magnificent healing work that God is doing in my life. It was then I realized the stone had been rolled away.

I was no longer suffocating with the physical effects of grief. My faith was becoming my sight. All of the promises that God had been revealing to me were being realized. I felt alive again.

My husband has been gone for a couple years now. In many cases, it feels like it was just yesterday. In other ways, I feel like he's been in the arms of Jesus for much longer. In either case, God's work of healing in my life has been nothing short of miraculous.

I have openly grieved...

I've grieved through this blog...

I've grieved through my own website...

I've grieved through social media...

I've grieved at church and amongst friends and family...

I've grieved with my counselor...

I've grieved in my own quiet spaces...

I've grieved alone and surrounded by friends.

I've grieved very hard. I have not hidden myself from the grief-work I've needed to do, and I truly believe that's why God has allowed my healing to manifest itself so vividly, so wholly, and, many ways, so quickly. That does not diminish the fact that this will be a lifelong process, but the pain has lessened, the light is much brighter, and I not only know that I have hope, but I feel hope all around me!

Christ's death was not the end...only the beginning...the tomb is empty...He is RISEN!

In a similar way, my husband's death was not the end of me...it brought a new beginning...the tomb of my grief is empty...and I, too, will one day rise to my permanent home in Heaven, and I will stand at death's funeral. Yes, death will die!

Until that time, I press onward, I run the race and I praise Him for carrying me through these months. My sisters, I pray that the stone before your "tomb of grief" will one day roll away before your very eyes, and when you "step outside" for that first breath of new air, may you see the One that's been carrying you, comforting you, and loving you through each day of your grief journey!

## April 4

### It is Finished!

Elizabeth Dyer

*For the wages of sin is death, but the gift of God is eternal life in Christ Jesus our Lord.*
*Romans 6:23 NIV*

Redeemed. That's what was written across my phone's coupon app. I looked at the screen and thought of Easter. I thought, "How cool if we could just carry around with us a picture of ourselves with a red ink-stamp across it, saying, 'Redeemed'!"

We do. It is called the Bible!

I learned a word that makes me feel intelligent. Tetelestai. It is the Greek word Jesus used on the cross. I see it on rubber bracelets, wooden signs, tattoos, bumper stickers.

The word is used only twice in Scripture. Once by John and once by Christ Himself.

*Jesus said, It is finished. With that, He bowed His head and gave up His spirit. John 19:30 NIV*

It is finished.

**It.**

The "it" is payment. We have a debt and He alone had the ability to pay. Romans 6:23 tells us the wages of sin is death.

**Is.**

The "is" means right this moment, but lasting for eternity. Romans 6:23 goes on to say the gift of God is eternal life.

**Finished.**

Completed. All the ceremonial laws of the Old Testament are finished. The shadows and hidden meanings of the sacrifices were made clear. The work of redemption and salvation is satisfied.

During this Easter season, let's remember what is *finished* in us personally. The guilt of our sin has been paid for. We were *redeemed* like a coupon. Nothing else needs to be *accomplished*. I can't attend church enough. I can't be good enough. I can't sing beautifully enough. I can't do **anything** enough. It is all His work on the cross.

As you see the cross displays during this Easter time, use your "spiritual glasses" to see *Tetelestai* written on each one. Remind yourself, "It is finished." Examine your heart today, making sure you are depending solely on His work and not your own for salvation. No more works. No more family lineage. No more sacrifices. Jesus Christ redeemed *you*. He did all that was required.

*Father God, You love me more than I can even begin to fathom. You allowed Your Son to pay the cost of redemption. I want to see the words Jesus spoke on the cross, "It is finished", written everywhere this Easter season. It is finished for my salvation. It is finished for my eternal life. It is finished for my relationship with Christ. It is finished. Thank You, thank You, thank You. Amen*

## April 5

## Waiting on Spring

By Liz Anne Wright

> *You will go out in joy*
> *and be led forth in peace;*
> *the mountains and hills*
> *will burst into song before you,*
> *and all the trees of the field*
> *will clap their hands.*
>
> *Isaiah 55:12 NIV*

Spring had finally sprung here in my hometown. A riot of color had burst forth, first from the Bradford Pears and then from the cherry trees. Beauty everywhere…except my little cherry tree in the yard.

Oh, she had plenty of buds. But nothing had opened yet. We had had some warm days, so I expected her to open, but she just hadn't. The other evening I was staring out the front window, pondering this. I am not sure what was so poignant about her standing there ready to bud, but it was. I was so moved by her standing there bud-filled-but-bloomless that I nearly took a picture.

The next morning, as the sun began to rise, I glanced out the window and could tell, even in the half-light of a dawning day, she had bloomed overnight. Just like that.

As the sun continued to rise, I watched my little tree and saw that nearly all those buds I had seen the day before had sprung open. This time, I did take a picture.

How, like my cherry tree, am I!

In this season of life, I often feel all-buds and no-bloom.

I have grieved fully and well these past five and a half years. I am sure I have more grieving to do (I don't know that I will be ever *totally* done), but for now, I am striding forward as *Liz* and no longer as *Keith's widow*.

I feel as though I am ready for new and more things, the next phase of my life. But God, in His infinite wisdom, knows when the *best* time for my next phase is.

I had a conversation with a dear friend the other night, and she said that sometimes she is itching to start some new phase in her life to God's glory, but has to wait a while to get the clearance from Him to get started. Like my budding tree, she sits and anticipates the spring, but with no bursting forth of direction. Then, suddenly, all the pieces fall into place, and God is ready for her to act. Again, like my little tree, she bursts forth to shine for His glory.

This is how I am choosing to view this season in my life--the dormancy before the spring bloom. God knows when I will burst forth. And I pray as I face each situation, I will trust in Him to know my perfect time to bloom.

In the myriad of decisions I now face alone, it is good to know I do not have to have all the answers.

Living in expectancy isn't always easy, but the fruit of waiting on the Lord, even in the new phases of this widow journey, will make it worth it.

*Lord, some days are hard to wait on You. I know You have the perfect plan and will reveal all the pieces of my new life when the time is right. Give me the strength to wait on You in all the areas of this widow-walk. In Jesus' name, Amen.*

## April 6

## We Are the Kingdom of God

By Sheryl Pepple

*Once, having been asked by the Pharisees
when the kingdom of God would come,
Jesus replied, "The kingdom of God does not come
with your careful observation,
nor will people say, 'Here it is,' or 'There it is,'
because the kingdom of God is within you."*
Luke 17:20-21 MSG

It has happened twice in my life. A pain so excruciating I could do nothing but pace in circles like a rabid animal. Once was a physical pain, the result of a serious side effect of a spinal tap. The second time, an emotional pain as the initial shock of my husband's death started to subside and the reality started to sink in. I can remember pacing in circles for hours that night, a deeply embedded instinct to try and escape the pain. A pain, so horrific, I knew I would never survive.

And yet, I have survived, not by my strength, but by His. He has captured every tear. More tears than I ever could have imagined. He has comforted me, He has provided for me, He has blessed me in so many ways. I live in His presence. I am His kingdom.

Often, when our husband passes away, we wonder, now that I am not a wife, what is my purpose? We lose sight of the bigger picture, of why we were created. We were created in the image of God, to glorify God. We were created to be the body of Christ, with Christ as the head. We were created to be the kingdom of God. And once we believe, *we are the kingdom of God.*

I have been immersed in the gospels lately and I have been reminded that far too often we forget the full implications of the Good News. We tend to think of the Good News as being the promise when we die, we will go to heaven, if we believe. But what we have been given is so much more than that. Christ lives in us and we are, right here, right now, the kingdom of God.

When Christ was on Earth in the flesh, His ministry was to preach and to heal people. Everywhere He went, He transformed lives. He ushered in the kingdom of God. Now He is on Earth inside us, and we are His kingdom in action. We are His hands and feet as He continues to minister and to share the Good News. He does it through us. What a privilege, what an amazing purpose, for our lives.

But what about the days we sit and sob all day? Or, the days we snap at everyone we know because we are so angry about the circumstances we find ourselves in? Or, what about the days when we pace in circles because of the horrific pain we are in?

Three years have passed since the night I spent hours pacing in circles because of the pain. I have seen His faithfulness. I have seen how He has drawn others to Him as He ministered to them through the kingdom of God - using my hands and feet.

I still have sad days. I still miss the physical presence of my husband by my side. But each day, I find great joy because **the kingdom of God is in me.** *Dear Heavenly Father, thank You for the reminder that You created me for Your kingdom. Help me be Your light to other widows to see Your goodness in my life. Father, may Your will be done on Earth as it is in Heaven. In Your Son's Holy and Precious Name. Amen*

## April 7

### Silencing a Storm

By Kit Hinkle

*Jesus reprimanded the disciples,*
*"Why are you such cowards, such faint-hearts?"*
*Then he stood up and told the wind to be silent,*
*the sea to quiet down: "Silence!"*
*The sea became smooth as glass.*
*Matthew 8:26 MSG*

Can you imagine a simple birthday making a coward of me? But it could. It would have been my husband Tom's fiftieth birthday.

One of my friends told me, "Most widows would spend the day trying to forget about it.... you're always so different! So I never know if I should be thinking that it was all roses for you, or if I should be worried about you??!!!"

Absolutely there are roses- with thorns of pain- but there is joy in knowing that I'm embracing challenges as they come up.

I so get why a widow would prefer to just forget about her husband's birthday. Daunting feelings of loss leap out at you, stinging you just the way it did when you first found out that you'd lost him forever.

Forgetting about a significant day doesn't work for kids or for me - it just pushes the terror of loneliness beneath the surface where it will bubble up in other ways.

As I looked at my four boys, who so loved to celebrate life with Dad, I knew exactly what I needed to do. Not run from that storm – *silence it!* Deal with it openly and honestly.

So the boys and I had a plan. We included crafts, a visit to the grave site, a hike and pizzeria outing, a bike ride, and a movie rental.

The day started very sad and awkward. Some of the boys broke into tears at the smallest of their errors, as though the entire work of art was now unworthy of Dad's approval. We all knew what the tears were about – what was ruined wasn't the card or craft, but the reality of not having Dad with them here on earth.

Their tears dried and they became more resolute in their artwork when convinced that Dad sees everything through the eyes of Christ now. Imperfections in the artwork are simply evidence of the love and joy in the children's hearts.

We brought the crafts to the site where Tom is buried and flew a model airplane there. There were also silly string battles, bubbles, and a round of "Happy Birthday to You" to celebrate. We went hiking about a mile away from our house to a pizza restaurant. This was something Tom did with them a lot. They had a blast getting muddy in the red clay "quick sand" and climbing mud hills.

We rented a movie, got donuts, and hiked back home.

Then it was time to pull out the bikes. We had them all repaired just for Tom's birthday. And Christian taught himself to ride a bike just this weekend. We rode on our neighborhood trail and on our cul-de-sac. Something so simple, but the kids LOVED it!

Then we settled down with the movie and sang Happy Birthday once more with the donuts in place of a cake.

The kids went to bed content that we honored Dad in a "Tom" kind of way.

The storm was silenced.

*Thank you, Lord, for answering our obedience to celebrate with joy rather than to cower in defeat. Amen*

## April 8

## Mommy Manna

By Danita Hiles

Somewhere in between the funeral and the first day of forever, there comes a point when you realize you are really doing this life alone. When you lie in bed and wonder if you really did lock the back door, and know **you** have to get up to check. When you sit in a school performance trying to clap louder and smile big enough to make up for the fact that Daddy isn't there. When you lose it the morning of leaving for vacation simply because your brain is exploding with all of the details you alone are in charge of. It is moments like this when I'm sure there just isn't enough mommy to go around.

That word 'enough' has come to mean a lot to me. God's Word promises that we have exactly what we need for the day He has given us. I **can** do this – today. He has promised us 'enough'- for today.

God established a plan for His day-by-day provision for the Israelites. At the beginning of every day, He promised enough manna for that day. The word manna means "portion"; it was the daily portion of what God had allotted for them, what He knew they needed. But as He repeatedly told the Israelites – they had to gather new manna each day. (Exodus 16: 16-18) Sure, He supernaturally provided it, but they had two responsibilities: 1. Gather it and 2. Eat, or appropriate it for today.

I think the commands are similar for us as widows:

1. Gather it: **Get into** His Word. **Fill** your mind with good stuff. **Spend time** with Him *before* the demands of the day take over. **Memorize** key verses that will help in moments of crisis. **Post** them so that you are surrounded by His truth.

2. Appropriate it: What are we going to do with what He has given us? **Choose** to respond instead of simply reacting. Take a **breath**, whisper a **prayer**, give yourself a **time-out**, whatever it takes. **Go to Him** first, and He will help you respond with wisdom instead of reacting out of emotion.

The simple truth of our daily reality is that many things simply will not look the same as they used to. We have to "wrap" our brains around new ways of taking vacations and having dinner and getting through after-school meltdowns.

When the days are long and the nights are longer, and you ache to be held just one more time – there is enough manna for that.

It is like a video game when your power runs low, a message flashes up on the screen saying, 'Your manna has been depleted'.

Can you relate? Sometimes it is time to just say, 'Lord, my manna has been depleted. I'm all out. Done. Finished.' Sometimes, it's just time for bed. I pray after a long day you can snuggle down for the night confident that there will be a fresh portion of manna, set out just for you, waiting tomorrow morning. Knowing there will again, be just enough of exactly what you need for whatever the day holds.

*Lord, thank You that when I am "done", You are right there to pick up the pieces of a long day. I trust You with my today and can go to sleep knowing You go before my tomorrow. Amen*

## April 9

### I'm Not Who I Was

By Nancy Howell

Not many months ago, I spent many hours of my life as a carefree married wife and mother. The next day, my husband had "routine" surgery. Five excruciatingly-long days later, I became a widow.

I look back at that forth-eight year old woman today, and I hardly recognize her. I'm not who I was.

I had the world on a string. My husband was my best friend, the love of my life. We worked to build our home and our marriage around God. We had two boys that we adored. We attended church, were involved in community and faith-based activities, and were counting down the days when my husband could take full retirement from his state job. We would head north to family farm-land in Kansas, where pasture acreage and a freshly-dug pond awaited us. Life was sweet.

Then he died.

And although I couldn't see it at the time, that's where my transformation began.

Twenty months later, with the gift of hindsight, I see differences. I have more grey hair. There's ten extra pounds on my frame, most likely from "grief eating." There are a few more wrinkles on my face.

But those are just the physical changes, all in outward appearance.

The inward transformation has been painstakingly beautiful, with the emphasis on "pain."

Here are just a few:

I am more patient.

I am more confident, making decisions as the head of my family and household.

I am more empathetic, and can cry at a moment's notice.

I am stronger than I thought I was.

I know first-hand how short life can be, and I cram every bit of fun I can into each day God gives me.

I forgive more easily.

I love more enormously.

I say what I mean, and I mean what I say.

I thirst after God, and try to seek His input on every aspect of my family's lives.

Am I perfect? Heavens, no! Am I healed? Not by a long shot.

I'm still under construction, thankful that God has great patience.

The important thing for widows to remember is this: **we must live our lives in such a way that there is only one death.** Those of us left must find purpose in some form or fashion, so that two people don't die (one physically, one emotionally) in the process.

God can take our grief and use it to transform us into women who can make a difference in others' lives, if we are willing to be refined and changed.

*God is keeping careful watch over us and the future. The Day is coming when you'll have it all--life healed and whole.*

*I know how great this makes you feel, even though you have to put up with every kind of aggravation in the meantime.*

*Pure gold put in the fire comes out of it* **proved** *pure; genuine faith put through this suffering comes out* **proved** *genuine.*

*When Jesus wraps this all up, it's your faith, not your gold, that God will have on display as evidence of his victory.*

*1 Peter 1:5-7 MSG*

What will we become through the test of fire? Only God knows. He's the one holding the blueprints.

*Father God, thank You for loving me, for walking beside me through my grief, my transformation, and my daily struggles. Give me the strength to be refined by the trials in my path. Don't let my grief be for nothing. Incorporate it into my soul with Your transforming powers, making me a better Christian, mother, daughter, and friend. You alone have the power. You alone have my love. In Jesus' name I ask it all, Amen.*

## April 10

## Small Beginnings

By Jill Byard

> *If you are faithful in little things,*
> *you will be faithful in larger ones...*
>
> *Luke 16:10 NLT*

One of the hardest emotions I have had to work through since the loss of my husband is the feeling of being insignificant and small. I will be honest and tell you this is not a new emotion. I have had this wrestling match in some form or another throughout my life. It seems the loss has ignited those emotions like oxygen when it wafts through a fire.

In the books of Matthew and Luke, Jesus speaks about the importance of the small in our world. While reading these passages, I realized in God's upside-down kingdom, beautiful always starts out small.

The mustard seed that Jesus refers to in several of his parables is extremely small. The average size of a mustard seed is 1.5mm-1.8mm. This means that one mustard seed is slightly bigger than the head of a pin. Yet, Jesus declares "if we have faith the size of a mustard seed we can move mountains or tell a tree to uproot itself and be planted in the sea." That is powerful!

Even though the mustard seed is minute, it contains every vital piece of information it needs to become a bush so tall that it can be mistaken for a tree. That amazes me!

Ponder these examples in our world:

The oak tree owes its beginning to an acorn.

A bonfire owes its beginning to a single spark.

A snowbank owes its beginning to a single snowflake.

A community changed owes its beginnings to a small act of kindness.

A legacy continued owes its new beginning to a woman who moves forward despite the pain.

God knows the importance of processing from small to great builds faith and develops strong foundations. Often the greatness is not instantaneous. It is a mere glimpse of what *can* happen when the small around us or in us stays faithful to the calling.

The next time small and insignificant emotions show their face to spar with me in the wrestling ring, I have a plan of action. I am going to start thinking about God's "upside-down kingdom", and see what He is trying to build in me. Choosing to take those emotions and use them as a reminder to be faithful to the calling. I want His greatness to be on display in me.

*Dear Lord, please help me on this road of widowhood. Help me remember when we are feeling small and insignificant, You have provided every single thing I need for my journey forward. I want to be faithful so Your greatness can be on display in every aspect of my life. In Your mighty name, Amen.*

## April 11

## Which Life Coach Will You Choose?

By Kit Hinkle

> *The thief comes only to steal and kill and destroy.*
> *I came that they may have life and have it abundantly.*
>
> *John 10:10 ESV*

The "thief" can fool us widows into twisting our grief in the wrong direction.

How does he do that? What would Christ have me do with my grief instead?

Grief is critical for moving forward. It's important to experience it and have patience with the time it takes to process your loss. But I've learned to distinguish between the *healthy* process of grieving and the signals the *thief* has come to steal my future using the pain of my loss.

**1. *The thief coaches you into "analysis paralysis". Christ comforts you and then coaches you to comfort others.*** In the first years of grief, I prayed and journaled about my loss, and talked through feelings with a confidant. All that gave me godly healing and comfort. There came a time, though, I found myself tempted to isolate, as though "thinking through" my loneliness would solve it. My pastor suggested I try something different— reach out and help someone lonelier than me. Soon I forgot my own problems and found myself lifted and fulfilled.

**2. *The thief coaches busyness for comfort. Christ coaches purposeful action—with prayer and time with Him topping your action list.*** At first, I found myself consumed with the desire to organize my house. Some of it was healthy, some not. I had to discern when *God* was calling me to put order to something, something that was interfering with moving forward in my life, and when I was simply rearranging the *clutter* just to get my mind off of grief. The thief whispered to me, "Stay busy, it doesn't matter that you're not accomplishing anything—just stay busy." Christ says, "…my yoke is easy, and my burden is light." (Matthew 11:30) Christ knows how He designed you and what actions bring fulfilling accomplishments rather than futile busyness.

**3. *The thief says to go to the phone. Christ says to first go to the throne.*** I have those moments when the phone isn't ringing and I'm surrounded only by my kids. I long for adult companionship. My first thought is to call someone. Christ says, "Come to Me, all who are weary." When I check in with Him, sometimes He encourages me to call a godly sister-in-Christ. Many times He, Himself, frees me from the weariness so I don't even *need* to use the phone at all.

**4. *The thief rushes you into life changes. Christ shows you He's enough for now.*** Our world is so coached by the enemy who wants you to believe in quick fixes. The Lord promises to defend the widow (Psalm 68:5). If you first learn to accept his lordship in your life and walk alone with him for a time, you'll find that later you'll be better prepared to take on an earthly husband again, if God allows it.

**5.** *The thief tells you to be afraid. Christ commands you not to fear.* Many of us resist the temptation to jump into relationships to the point we then feel most comfortable on our own. We wonder what might go wrong if we consider another marriage. Those concerns are healthy as long as we don't let the enemy twist those into consuming fear. Far from being the author of fear, Christ tells us on five occasions in the Book of John not to fear.

What have you found as signals that you need to turn to Christ?

*Dear Lord, show me in these seasons of weakness, no matter how difficult and testing, You teach me to lean on You. Help me learn that, by leaning on You, I become closer to who You made me to be. Amen.*

## April 12

## How To Fill A Gap

By Liz Anne Wright

*Carry each other's burdens, and in this way
you will fulfill the law of Christ.*
*Galatians 6:2 NIV*

Five o'clock was the hardest time. My sweet husband had always walked in the door at five. On the dot.

My day of doing this thing called "parenting" on my own had ended. I had some backup. I had someone to give me a hug and kiss, listen to how my day was, and take a bit of burden from my shoulders.

After he was gone, five o'clock was the hardest.

At first, I tried to carry on in the same way, having dinner on the table at five, the way he always liked it. But, it quickly became too much for me.

Enter my sweet friend, Susan.

Her family is one of those that does not eat dinner until 7:30-8:00 due to her husband's work schedule. She had finished her homeschool day, but was not quite ready to start cooking dinner. She had time to talk.

And talk we did! Every day about 5:00, we would be on the phone, just chatting about the day, what the kids had done, what had been hard, what had been joyous...many of the things I would have shared with Keith, if he had been here.

This continued for quite a while. She was there for me, every day at the same time, the time when I needed her most. She shared some of her day and struggles as well, but her primary interest was helping me through a tough time of day. It was a gift and a blessing.

And I know she *prayed*. She prayed for me in my grief, prayed for my own walk with Christ through this time, prayed for my kids and our homeschool world. That was the greatest part of the gift - the investment she put into me and my family on her knees.

As time wore on, and the grief was not so raw, I found that I was not so *down* each day at five. It got a bit easier to get dinner on the table without missing Keith. I fell into a new routine, became comfortable with my new place in life.

Susan and I are still close. She is one of those special friends who is in my life for the long haul, through whatever happens to each of us...and I praise God for that.

Sisters, as widows we have great needs. One can just be for conversation in the midst of carpooling and cleaning and caring for kids. I pray that you each have a "Susan" in your life to help carry that burden. I pray that you have the strength to seek what you need in others, and the discernment to know when to lean on a friend. I pray that, in time, you can grow beyond the circumstances of your grief to *be* this friend to another, whether she is facing the same journey or not. I pray that you can lean on our loving Father in all the good times and the hard times, even when someone is not physically there with us.

*Dear Father, thank You for friends who have my back, who listen to my words, who walk beside me. I pray I can appreciate each and every one You give me, and that I can be that friend to others along the way. In Jesus' Name, Amen.*

## April 13

## The End of the Story

By Nancy Howell

*So we're not giving up. How could we?*
*Even though on the outside it often looks like things*
*are falling apart on us, on the inside, where God is making new*
*life, not a day goes by without his unfolding grace. These hard*
*times are small potatoes compared to the coming good times, the*
*lavish celebration prepared for us.*
*There's far more here than meets the eye.*
*The things we see now are here today, gone tomorrow.*
*But the things we can't see now will last forever.*

*2 Corinthians 4:16-18 The MSG*

Have you ever felt like giving up? Disconnecting the phones, crawling back into bed, pulling the covers over your head? I bet we've all been there. Some of us in this unimagined journey may be past this stage, while others may be right in the midst of it. Even though I rarely follow through on those thoughts, I still have days where a part of me wants to give in to the pain of widowhood by giving up and giving in.

But for me, really giving up was never an option. Although I had lost my husband, our two young sons looked expectantly to me to pick up the pieces and guide our family into the future.

So I did what any other mother in my position would do--I forged ahead. There were days I did not have a clue as to what I was doing. I made decisions based solely on prayer and intuition. Slowly but surely

I began to feel more confident in making head of household decisions, with only God to consult with.

On the outside, it may have seemed like life was falling apart all around us. Plans and dreams that were in the works for the Howell family of four had to be reevaluated and re-assessed. Some we had to let go of completely, and that was difficult. Others we are continuing to follow. The rest are in a state of flux and uncertainty as we await God for direction. The Howell family of three is slowly regrouping, once again finding purpose in life.

For you see, even on the worst of days, God is still at work within us. He's been beside me on the rough days, days I didn't think I could make it until the next minute. He's curled up beside me on nights where it seemed I could never go to sleep in my big bed alone, after sharing it with a spouse for almost twenty-three years.

He's helped me make decisions for my family, for our future, by giving me counsel and guidance, the best I could ever hope to have. He's given me glimpses of joy and happiness, when I thought those were emotions I might never feel again.

Most importantly He has showed me that really bad circumstances can build character, empathy, and faith. I never thought good could come from such bad, but thanks to God, it has.

The end of my husband's life could've been the end of my story--and it would've been a pretty good one to tell. But God tells me I still have purpose. I have work to do for Him, joy to experience, sons to raise, songs to sing, books to write.

He is enough. You, too, have a purpose. Don't give up. Your story should not end with the death of your spouse. There's so much more that God wants to help you write.

*Father God, I pray that I feel the all-encompassing love and grace that You and only You can provide. Fill in the cracks of my brokenness, let me see my story hasn't ended just because I lost a spouse. In many ways, it's just beginning. I want to find purpose in this new uncharted territory of widowhood, so that Your kingdom will be glorified. Because You make all things new. Amen*

## April 14

### From Sea to See

By Julie Wright

> *Teacher, do You not care that we are perishing?*
> *Mark 4:38 ESV*
> *"Why are you so afraid? Have you still no faith?" And they were filled with great fear and said to one another, "Who then is this, that even the wind and the sea obey him?"*
> *Mark 4:40-41 ESV*

"I'm lonely."

"I don't understand why God would let this happen."

"I never imagined my life like this."

"I can't do this alone. It's hard and it hurts so much still."

Have you said anything like this? I can relate to all the pain, sadness, loneliness and loss of control. I too stood in that valley covered in tears, questions, and fear. I knew in my head what was true, right and best, but my heart just wasn't connecting the dots. If one more person called me "inspirational" or such a "testimony" I thought I would punch them. How Christ-like is that reaction?

I remember thinking, "Really? Inspirational? Come to my house late at night. Look at me curled up in the bed unable to sleep and crying so hard that I thought my chest would collapse. Peek in on me in the morning when the sun peers through the window and my first thought is, great....another day without him."

So, after reading sifting through my journals from the past two and a half years, I wanted to know what changed. What caused me to go from a curled up ball on my bed each night for weeks on end to a widow who stands tall and confident (on most days)?

Jesus. That's my answer, Jesus.

We trod along with our perfect lives, our loving husband and adoring kids. Then one day, out of the blue or maybe slowly over time, that life is eroded or turned on its side...all the contents scattered and tossed out on a sea of grief we never thought we would experience.

That's when we begin to question God. Do you see me? Do you care? Do you see my children and their sadness? Can you hear my cries and groans?

After all the tears were wiped away and my vision became clearer, I knew deep down in my heart that Jesus loved me. He was with me IN my circumstances. God had felt them himself. God knows how I feel. He watched His only Son die on the cross for me...for me. Even Jesus cried out to God, "Why have you forsaken me? Why have you forgotten me?"

The whole earth became dark that day. God's grief was just like mine. Dark, hard, painful.

But then, Jesus conquered the grave. He arose and helped us to "see" that although this life is tough, painful and sad at times, this earthly life is not the end. There is HOPE. There is LOVE. There is JESUS. Although he brings grief, he will show compassion, so great is his unfailing love.

Jesus; the name that casts out all fear, doubt and loneliness. The name that heals our hearts, our minds and gives us the strength we need for each day.

My prayer is that you will be able to "see" one day soon, past the "sea" of grief that surrounds you and know that you are loved, you are special and that the HOPE of eternity is near. Jesus, Jesus, Jesus…feel him near.

## April 15

### A Mess

By Erika Graham

*Then Jesus said, "Come to me all who are weary and carry heavy burdens, and I will give you rest.*
*Take my yoke upon you. Let me teach you,*
*because I am humble and gentle at heart,*
*and you will find rest for your souls."*

*Matthew 11:28-29 NLT*

As I frantically ran around chucking things into closets and behind doors I could keep closed, my husband yelled from the kitchen his thoughts on the matter. He couldn't believe anyone was really going to care what my house looked like, and wasn't sure why I cared so much.

I was hosting a last minute get together with a few friends and their kids. But, twin boys under age two, didn't lend to a super-clean house most days. My husband was right, I shouldn't care. Yet, I didn't want anyone else knowing, even as a stay-at-home mom, I struggled to keep up on the house stuff. So, I ran around hiding the evidence.

Those frantic moments of trying to clean up, came to mind often after my husband passed, because there were days where my house was an even greater mess than it ever had been back then. There were dishes in the sink, laundry piled up, and disarray everywhere.

I called those our "ugly" days, and I would phone or text friends and ask for prayer when they hit us. As we did the "grief thing", some days were just so very tough. Those days, we would just hunker down at home, ignore the to-do list, and we would just be.

We'd snuggle.

We'd cry.

We'd remember.

We'd pray. Asking God to just sit with us, love us, speak into us words of healing, and we would just go to Him.

I realize now those days were the most precious ones. The physical mess around us, honestly paled in comparison to the mess we had going on inside us.

Those moments together have become some of my most treasured memories, post loss.

My kids won't remember if I did the laundry, the dishes, or the other chores. But, they will remember how I "did" grief. They'll remember I was there to hold them, to cry with them, to wipe their tears, to reassure them, and to remember with them. They will remember God met us there and He spoke into us during those ugly days. They saw and felt Him comfort and heal us.

They can see and recognize that *now*, because we took the time *then*. We went to HIM and He met our needs.

Sisters, leave your house a mess. It's okay some days. Don't miss the moments, don't lose the chances. If you have children, they need you most now. If you don't or yours are launched, there are still others who need you, and the care and understanding you can exude because of your own loss. Take the time to minister to those around you in the midst of your own "tough stuff". The lessons and blessings exceed anything you can imagine. And the testimony you will be, will reveal how amazing God is in our suffering.

*Father God, continue to heal me and move me forward, revealing what You would have me pour into others around me. Heal my heart through times of rest, and release me from the burden of being everything to everyone. Help me recognize the important stuff in life and embrace it, even if it means letting the house be a mess, or chores and errands go undone. In Your Matchless Name, Amen.*

## April 16

## Letting Go

By Karen Emberlin

*The LORD will work out His plans for my life.*

*Psalm 138:8 TLB*

For the past three years, since my husband's home going, I have still considered where we last lived in Tennessee, as "home". It is the place where everything is familiar, where I remember our home - filled with our "stuff", our friends, our church, favorite restaurants, favorite stores, and many memories. We loved the mountains - this was where we were going to grow old together!

After my husband's sudden and unexpected passing, it was very evident that I could not function in Tennessee on my own; I needed to be closer to my family. On the second move in the first year, I moved a tiny amount of our "stuff" back to the mid-west, where I grew up.

This year, as I approached the third anniversary of my husband's passing, I had a very strong urge to get back "home" to Tennessee. I knew getting back "home" would be a bit of a challenge. It would be a seven hour drive (which I could not do alone) and there were no good air connections. I continued to pray something would work out. My cousin called to say she and her husband were planning some time away, and would be driving within miles of where I wanted to go. Perfect timing!

I believe the time back "home" was a significant part of the healing process for me. I had a wonderful time with old friends. We reminisced, went back to our favorite restaurants and stores, our church, and I even went back to see our home and neighborhood. Most things have not changed, but I began to realize that *even if I could go back just like it was, it would never be the same without my husband!* The things I long for and remember include him – without him in the picture, it would never be the same.

*Admitting and really believing that my husband is gone, and life's got to go on is probably one of the toughest things I have ever done.* When you love someone so deeply (in my case for nearly fifty years) and he had filled a need that was never filled by anyone else, letting go is not easy.

I was very grateful to be back "home" on the third anniversary of my husband's death. Yes, there were moments of sadness and some tears, but I was also able to smile and know in my heart that my husband's purpose on earth was fulfilled when God called him "home".

Even though my life was suddenly changed, I know God has a purpose and a plan for me too. He created me to fulfill that purpose and has left me here on earth to do that, *but* I must desire His plan for "my" life now.

My physical address and location may have changed, but I will never forget the time we lived in Tennessee. I will continue to go back and visit this special place, and in my heart I will always consider it my "home" until He calls me to my final "home" with Him!

*Lord God, I know things will never be the same again, and I will never be able to go back to the way they were. I admit this, Lord. I ask You to help me to move forward with excitement and a purpose, seeking to fulfill Your plan for my life. Amen.*

## April 17

## It Matters For the Kingdom

By Lori Reynolds Streller

I stand staring at the photo on our kitchen counter.

I'm lost in the memory.

*It was a party. We are sitting together on the ottoman in our friend's living room, snuggled close and laughing. Our friend turns around with her camera and instantly Tim comes in for a kiss, and then pretends to licmayk my face instead. We are wrestling and laughing, then settling back in tightly together for the photo.*

My mind rushes to the day this friend showed up at our home eight months later with the beautifully framed photograph of that moment. A gift received after my husband's diagnosis. It's the photo I am transfixed on now.

*How, God? How does it happen? This death thing; the "here one second and gone the next"? I don't understand.*

I am paralyzed in place, just staring in wonder.

My brain cannot process the reality that he is gone. Although I am living with that very real truth day in and day out, there is just something so surreal about the permanency of it.

Memories bombard my thoughts, emotions wash over me in waves so strong if I close my eyes I am easily lost and can almost feel Tim's presence in them.

Dinner sizzles in the skillet I have neglected. Still, I cannot pull myself away from the photograph.

*Lord, give me wisdom. Teach me to number my days.* (Psalm 90:12)

*Why did you take Tim and leave me? Oh, God, wash over me with Your peace!*

*James 3:17-18 NIV But the wisdom that comes from heaven is first of all pure; then peace-loving...*

So full of tears my vision cannot focus, my eyes finally pull themselves away from the photograph. I lean in, elbows on the counter, head dropped low, gently rocking back and forth.

*Father, I don't understand the how or the why, but I trust You. I am incapable of wrapping my feeble human brain around the death process. I can't comprehend the minuteness of this life in Your timetable of eternity. I will choose to thank You. I will choose to surrender. I will choose to allow You to use my pain for Your glory.*

*1 Peter 1:6 NIV In this you greatly rejoice, though now for a little while you may have had to suffer grief in all kinds of trials. These have come so that your faith—of greater worth than gold, which perishes even though refined by fire—may be proved genuine and may result in praise, glory and honor when Jesus Christ is revealed.*

*Lord, refine me. Prove my faith as genuine. Receive all praise, glory and honor. Amen.*

Ladies, I want you to know that it is okay to ask God the **hard** questions. It is okay to not understand the details of our Master's plan. I am just as confused as you are as to the whys and the how of this widow life. I will not pretend for one second that it is easy to fully surrender with a thankful heart. It takes a disciplined and deliberate choice, sometimes moment by agonizing moment. And grief, well, it likes to slam into us when we least expect it. I was simply cooking dinner, when this photograph that has graced our kitchen counter for over two years now caught my eye in a new way.

Unexpected grief.

There is comfort in our queries. There is wisdom in our seeking. There is peace in the imperfection of this life. It is all found in our surrender to God. One day, we will stand before the King of Kings and all of this will make sense and it **will** matter. **We** matter. Our pain and our grief will have **mattered**. **It matters for the kingdom, whether we understand it or not.**


## April 18

**Our Hearts, Your Will**

By Erika Graham

> *The heart of man plans his way,*
> *but the Lord establishes his steps.*
> *Proverbs 16:9 ESV*

I'm five years into my widowhood, so there's routine, there's new traditions, there's joy, and renewed celebration of holidays. But, it's never ever going to be the same. It still stinks and there's still a void. It will always be tough!

For a recent vacation, I decided we needed something to kick it off well. I weighed many options and landed on Hershey, PA, the self-proclaimed "Sweetest Place on Earth". We arrived, and our room had a balcony overlooking the indoor pool. The kids immediately begged to go swimming.

As I sat there watching my three kids frolic and play together, I noticed everyone in the pool above the age of eighteen was male. Then it hit me--they're all

DADS! I watched as the dads threw their kids into the pool and played with their kids. I listened as the kids squealed in delight, "Daddy watch me, Daddy catch me, Daddy throw me!"

I glanced over at one of my sons, who was also just standing, frozen, watching. He saw me looking, walked over to me and just threw himself into my arms. He was reminded like I was, that one family member was missing. His own daddy!

Later, my boys wanted to throw change into the hotel fountain, so I gave them each three pennies instructing them to make three wishes. They ran over, eagerly stood and contemplated their wishes, then gleefully threw their money in.

In our room for the night, the boys quietly whispered, "Mommy, we know it's bad luck, but we want to share our biggest wish with you." As I told them I would love to hear their wishes, they continued, "Well, we both decided, we want a new daddy to play and have fun with here on earth. That's our biggest wish!"

Youch, a punch right in the grief gut.

Tears flowed freely and quickly, as I told them how much I loved them and how much their irreplaceable daddy loved them. They just long for a physical guy to meet their needs. They want to be tossed in the air, and loved, and paid attention to by some great guy. I get it!

We prayed together for the "new" God has in store for us ahead, and, yes, we even prayed for a "new" man to come into our life. Not because we can't do it without someone. Because, God is certainly our all in all, He has become my Husband and my kids Father. But, there's still life left here. There's still eight year old boys who desire a man to teach them "boy" stuff. There's still a twelve year old girl who needs a man to teach her how she should be treated, what a Godly husband looks like. There's still a thirty-something woman who would love to share her life and have a partner again.

We know God can be trusted, and we petitioned Him for the things we desire. The important part is trusting Him, no matter what happens.

My kids and I ended that night, with our most favorite part of our prayer, *"Lord, not our will, but Yours. In Your Matchless Name, Amen."*


## April 19

### Letting Go of a Dream

By Elizabeth Dyer

> *I had it in my heart to build a house*
> *as a place of rest for the ark...*
> *And I made plans to build it.*
> *But God said, "You are not to build a house..."*
> I Chronicles 28:2-3 NIV

"You mean, I won't be the one, Lord?"

"No, David. You won't. You followed Me, you have a heart for Me, but this is not going to happen during your lifetime."

"But I dreamed of it! I planned it! I wanted this to be my ultimate gift to You, Lord."

"No, David. I have a different plan. I am going to hand the dream over to your son, Solomon. He is the man who will see the temple completed."

My dreams. My plans. All gone. This time I thought Yahweh and I were working pretty closely together.

I was drawing some amazing plans for a permanent home for the Ark of the Covenant. It was just so wrong for me to live in comfort when the Lord's property was sitting in a tent. I would wake up in the middle of the night with new and exciting ideas to include in the plan. I talked to God often about it. I planned every tiny detail – the courts, the treasuries, the job descriptions of the workers, even down to the weight of the gold and silver lampstands! God's hand was on me as He enabled me to understand all these details. We had some great plans! And He helped me MAKE the plans.

So when I was in prayer and meditation recently, I was so surprised what Yahweh shared with me. Who knows why I was even given the privilege of being the King over these people anyway. I was such a lowly shepherd boy from the tribe of Judah – of no real significance. My brothers were so much finer than I! Who can know the mind of God? But this was so much more difficult for me to accept. God and I had been through so much together – Battles. Near-death experiences. Sin. King Saul. I wanted so much to build this temple for God as a way of showing my appreciation and love and respect.

But God said my son Solomon, of all my sons, would be on the throne and would be making MY dream a reality. My dream.

How do you handle your dreams being ripped from your hands? During the dark hours of the night, do you struggle with the loss of your dreams? I had every right to this dream. Do you know what I mean?

Do you ever feel like your right to your dream was smashed? I know the feeling. How do you let go of the past dreams and anticipate God's work in the future with a renewed trust in Him?

When our dreams have to be released, we are given the opportunity to grow in our faith. When life doesn't make sense, we are given the opportunity to trust in our Creator more than ever in our lives. King David went on, in this chapter of 1 Chronicles 28, to tell all the Israelites what God had done in the past, how He had chosen the tribe of Judah specifically, and then handed over the "blueprints" to his son Solomon. He challenged Solomon to follow whole-heartedly, and told the entire gathering of Israelites that God had CHOSEN Solomon to fulfill King David's dream temple.

**Let's learn from King David's example in this passage that our dreams sometimes are given to another person to carry out or are just released into the atmosphere. How we respond determines how we will grow.**

*Father God, You were instrumental in so much of my dreams. You created the desire in me for these dreams. Help me release my past and accept the future, as I trust You like never before. Amen*

## April 20

## Out of Order

By Kit Hinkle

Sweet Sisters, I'd like to talk about one of my deepest failures as a widow. I guess what God lays on my heart to share with you usually has something to do with overcoming fear and struggles, and finding joy in my walk alone with the Lord.

But the reality of my flaws is as true as the reality of the confidence the Lord gives me, and I like that. It keeps me pathetic enough to keep leaning on Him for more confidence. And when I sat down to write today, one of these failures kept coming to mind, inviting me to tell you about it.

It's my failure to master household repairs. Year after year since losing Tom, items sink further into disrepair. Not total shambles, mind you. Come visit, and you'll notice it's kept neat, and, at first glance, you might even say I do quite well with the upkeep.

That's at first glance.

Look a little closer, and you'll start noticing things… a counter top cracked down the middle, a built-in microwave with an OUT OF ORDER sign on the door—the cheaper counter-top model taking up space underneath. A broken faucet drips in the guest bath. The keypad for the speaker system throughout the house blinks the same odd light for the past three years since the day it stopped working. It wasn't long after that keypad stopped working, when the intercom stopped functioning, and the doorbell started to buzz an odd sound of electrical fuzz instead of a sing-songy ding dong.

I'll stop with the list—you get the idea. These broken things are symptoms that half of me is missing—the half that always took care of the home.

Somewhere in my brain I haven't let go of the idea of having a man take care broken things. It's all just supposed to work, like it did before. Before Tom died. When something broke, he fixed it, by golly, and he didn't give up until it worked, even if it meant pulling out the duct tape or replacing the dumb thing.

Now, one by one, things are breaking in the house. And each time they do, I stare at it, blankly at first. I'd already experienced repairmen coming over and talking circles around me until I paid them exorbitant fees just to get them to leave and be done with all of it.

After all, do I really want to fix the counter? An estimator came out and told me it would require replacement of the cabinets underneath. Who knows whether he's telling the truth? Without a man around, he might be seeing me as an opportunity for some easy money.

And do I really want to call on friends for help? I'm thinking four years is about time to put away my widow card and handle things on my own. *But how I wish someone would help.* Bottom line is that my busyness and constant chasing to keep up with life keeps me from slowing down long enough to learn *how* and *when* to manage repairs.

It's a season, and unlike so many problems during this season that God's provided an answer for, this one goes without answer. And maybe that's His purpose for this struggle. In today's culture of perfectionism, we put so much pressure on ourselves to have it together in order to be acceptable.

**Sometimes failure allows us to recognize just how flawed we are and how much we need a Savior.**

Not all the matters of a widow come with answers. Sometimes it's part of the storm whirling around our lives, and the acceptance of our circumstances as part of the season brings the joy in the midst of struggle.

*Heavenly Father, help me know I am completely accepted by You, even if I am unable to keep up in certain areas of my life. Amen.*

## April 21

## Would He Recognize Me?

By Jill Byard

*For it is God who works in you to will and to act in order to fulfill His good purpose.*

*Philippians 2:13 NIV*

As time moves farther away from the day my husband became a resident of heaven, I often wonder if he would recognize the woman that he left behind.

He encouraged me to venture out beyond our little world. Sometimes I did venture beyond and other times, not so much. As I look back on our years together, I see how he and God were preparing me for the time when I would be the only gate-keeper in our family. Circumstances beyond our control, but fully known to our faithful God.

These ponderings have made me realize the beauty of God's unconditional love for me. He knows my strengths. He knows my weaknesses. He knows my failings. He knows my gifts. He knows all the things that leave me feeling like I don't measure up. He sees my frustrations while I maneuver through this new single parent life. He knows how I want to run during worship when I see couples holding hands at church. However, He chooses to love me simply because He created me. **He always keeps my purpose on his day planner.**

The way my God loves me and the way my David loved me worked together to prepare me for my future. God knew I would have to rely solely on His guidance and only recollections of David's wisdom.

I serve an exquisitely intentional God. He covers me so completely. He equips me for the things that haven't been made known to me yet. The mere thought of this leaves me speechless.

I have come to understand my David had confidence in my potential more than I ever did. He knew my failings. He chose to love me like Christ loved the church. He became my shield when hard times came knocking at our door and always honored me in front of our girls.

My God and my David always saw my potential and they have been trying to convince me of this fact for years. The only one who was surprised when I fixed my own hot water heater was myself. God planned that very day in advance and helped me like a daddy coaching a little league softball game. He leaned down and took notice. He had been waiting to see this event and anticipated seeing my confidence grow as I completed the task.

Sweet Sisters, as you venture out into unknown territory, please remember that you have been equipped for every encounter you face, every obstacle you encounter, and every hurdle you overcome. God made you to thrive in every circumstance. Often we look to see the progress in our efforts. We need to remember, if we are faithful, the process will ensure our continued progress.

*Dear Lord, Thank You for equipping me with everything I need to carry out Your purpose for my life. Thank You for Your unconditional love that never gives up on me. Thank You for the gift of my husband.. Thank You for showing me that my faithfulness to the process has value. Help me to live beyond my fears and embrace my future with confidence. In Your Mighty Name, Amen.*

## April 22

## A Glimmer of Hope

By Danita Hiles

My garage door broke recently. A few days ago I lifted the huge creaking door in order to walk the trash to the curb. Back in the garage, I reached up to drag the door down, down, down.

And then, darkness. Complete and utter darkness.

The door to the house had slammed shut behind me. Between me and that door was a twenty-five foot, pitch black, obstacle course of bikes and pool toys and coolers and lawn care tools. My eyes strained to adjust to the darkness and seek out any small liver of light. Suddenly this garage blackout experience felt a whole lot like my life.

I remembered the moment nine years ago when my once sweet, funny, handsome husband lay on an emergency room gurney. I remember the doctor's slow hesitant words, "We did everything we could, Mrs. Hiles." I remember the darkness that seemed to swallow me. A darkness so encompassing that I felt like I could barely breathe. I remember looking for the light, some light, any light to bring hope to this impossible reality.

Walking back into my home from the hospital nine years ago, little glimmers of light began to flicker in the darkness. Military paperwork that magically got sorted out by the right person at the right time. The wag of our dog's tail. Kisses from my girls. Phone calls and love and hugs at just the right time. Chicken enchiladas delivered on a particularly difficult day – Dave's favorite dish. Opening my Bible to a verse that shouted peace and provision and hope for the future. Glimmers of hope that God was still there and a new normal was maybe somehow possible.

Back to the present, standing in my dark garage. I was reminded of the same journey I walked through darkness nine years ago. Now, as then, I needed to do two things:

- **Go toward the light.** The only way to get of the dark garage was to walk toward the glimmer of light. There are things that continue to shine hope and peace into our days. Things that show us God's faithfulness and remind us of His truth. Seek Him through His Word daily. Look for things that you can choose to be thankful for, even something as simple as an early morning cup of coffee or air conditioning that works!

- **Remember what you know.** Just as I had to carefully navigate a cluttered garage by trying to remember where things were located, we need to remember what we know. **Even in the face of the impossible, God's truth is still God's truth**. It all really comes back to that children's prayer most of learned as a kid: 'God is great, God is good'. Do we really believe that? I know, I know, sometimes it is so hard! Me, too. I strongly urge you to start keeping a journal, and if you have one, go back and read of His faithfulness. (Psalm 27:1, Psalm 3:3, and Psalm 18:2-3)

Wherever you are in your journey, whether stumbling through smothering darkness or hesitantly walking in glimmers of light, know that He is with you....and that your sisters all over the world are shoulder to shoulder beside you as well. Now, if you'll excuse me, it's probably a good idea to get out there and clean out that garage!

*Lord, thank You that You are the Light of the world. You shine light on all our dark situations. May I establish my days on the Truth of Your Word instead of "roller coaster" emotions that derail my peace. Amen*

## April 23

## A New Name

By Leah Stirewalt

I have a little secret about my name. You see, it hasn't always been Leah. Granted that's the name on my birth certificate, but I have to confess that my name actually used to be Julie. As a matter of fact, I went by Julie. For a whole **day**. In Kindergarten, that is.

When I was a little girl, my parents shared with me that they *almost* named me Julie Diane instead of the name they ended up giving me at birth, Leah Kristen. I was just devastated to learn that I almost had been given the most beautiful, most enchanting name my little ears had ever heard up to that time…Julie Diane. Instead, I was Leah Kristen. "Boring," I thought.

One day, a new girl was enrolled in our kindergarten class. When she and I we were alone in the "puppet center" together, I took a moment to personally introduce myself to her and – of course – shared my name with her…Julie. Diane. I sure did. I lied right then and there, and I got away with it. Well, for the rest of that day, that is. The charade ended the next morning when the teacher took role, and "Julie Diane" didn't exist.

Many years ago, in the land of Canaan – the Promised Land – in the time of the Judges, there was another person who called himself by a different name. God's chosen people, the Israelites, had just been ravaged by the Midianites. The Israelites, once again, cried to God for mercy, and God was once again about to pour out mercy on them. He even had His battle leader already hand-picked. But, this was not just any battle leader...this was Gideon, a simple wheat thresher.

*Judges 6:11-16 NIV The angel of the Lord came and sat down under the oak in Ophrah that belonged to Joash the Abiezrite, where his son Gideon was threshing wheat in a winepress to keep it from the Midianites. When the angel of the Lord appeared to Gideon, he said, "The Lord is with you,* **mighty warrior.***"* (Emphasis mine)

Friends, God saw Gideon as He was making Him – into a mighty warrior. In the next chapter, God uses Gideon to totally defeat the Midianites. Gideon had a different name for himself – weak, the least, a simple wheat thresher. But **God turned Gideon's name of weakness into strength.**

Ladies, what name has God given you that you have yet to discover or take hold of? What name have you placed upon yourself that has crippled you? Are you pretending – like "Julie Diane" did that day many years ago? Or – are you choosing to walk by faith with your new name?

God revealed to me recently that I am very quick to apply names to myself, and typically those "names" I use are not edifying to Him.

Lonely. Lost. Confused. Scared. Abandoned. Rather He tells me I am...

Loved

Made in His image

Beautiful

His friend

Intimately known by Him

Never alone

Chosen

Free

...just to name a few.

On the days that grief is wearing you down and the enemy tries to tell you that you are defeated and that you will always feel this way, remind him who God says you are! Go to His Word, whisper His name, call out to Him and ask Him to call you by name. Own THAT name, dear ones. On the day when you feel as if the burden of grief is too great to bear, allow God's name for you to be your strength.

You are His treasure!

## April 24

### Inviting Others Into Your Healing Journey

By Kit Hinkle

*Religion that is pure and undefiled before God, the Father, is this: to visit orphans and widows in their affliction, and to keep oneself unstained from the world.*

*James 1:27 ESV*

People around you want to help and visiting you is one way they can. After all, James 1:27 tells people to visit you in your affliction.

The first few months after my husband Tom passed away, I was surrounded with sweet friends, family, cards, and phone calls. But after the second full year, my support system had waned. Can you relate?

God told the Israelites that He blesses those who bless them (Genesis 12:3a). While He directed this to the Hebrews, this text teaches us that *others* receive when they can bless *us*. As a widow, one way we can bless others is by making it **easy** for them to help you. Desiring for *others* to be blessed is the beginning of helping *you* get the help you need.

I have a suggestion—compile a Basket of Ten. A Basket of Ten is a simple technique designed to put the support needed for your healing process somewhat in your hands, so you take responsibility for it.

**Support is Critical:**

When you are in a serious phase of grieving, you can't deny it—you are emotionally needy. People understand your needs right after your loss, but few understand how long grief takes to process. In the second year, you still need a friend to talk to, one who won't judge you for still having tears.

**How It Works:**

1. **Cultivate a network** - Take ten people who love you and would be willing to occasionally drop everything to listen and love on you. Start with your family—your sister, mother, aunt, or cousin—because you know they love you. Then add friends. Next, acquaintances. Soon you'll find yourself keeping your eyes open for others to add to your Basket of Ten.

2. **Find the right number** - You don't need exactly ten. But you do have to have enough to maintain consistent, available support of healthy loved ones who respect you. With the ordeal you are going through, you will need help OFTEN. Having only a handful of support friends will not be enough.

3. **Never start with the same one** - Rotate the order you call people. If you talked with your sister yesterday, try your neighbor today. And if someone always seems too busy or not caring enough—perhaps it's just not a good fit. It isn't personal. Have grace with her and keep your eyes open for another.

**Fruits from the basket:**

After you've taken control of your healing, you'll feel empowered to move forward. Enjoy the fruits of your labor!

- Un-sour Grapes - Friends won't feel awkward because they haven't heard from you and think they've "dropped the ball" and neglected you. They know they are on your *list* and when you need them, they're honored to be there.
- Smiling Bananas - You are getting the support you need and feel better about your healing.
- Sweet Orange - Better on the inside. You'll develop deeper friendships based on more than just their occasional niceties.

The basket gives you a symbol of friends who will nourish you and sets guidelines for requesting their help with respect for their time. That type of boundary setting will carry on into your new season and set you on solid ground with friends.

*Dear Father God, I need Your love. Thank You for sending it through the hands, feet, and mouths of Your sons and daughters. Help me consider formalizing my process of reaching out so I can form safe, healthy friendships to grow me through this season of grief. Amen*

## April 25

### Unexpected

By Danita Hiles

I ran a race this weekend.

Pretty funny even writing those words because I am not a 'runner'. But Sunday morning at 5:00 am found me with 20,000 other crazy ladies (and a few brave guys) getting ready to start the Disney Princess Half Marathon. Yep, that's right. 13.1 miles.

Somewhere between the ball at Epcot and Cinderella's Castle, I realized this race felt a lot like life.

There is a course in front of us and each morning we get out there and face it. Although we are surrounded by thousands others, our race is an individual one. It is up to me to put one foot in front of the other, step by step, knowing that God is with me. Maybe that's why Paul talks so much about running in his writings. *Hebrews 12:1 "...let us throw off everything that hinders and the sin that so easily entangles, and let us run with perseverance the race marked out for us". NIV*

There were a lot of surprises in this race for me. I expected there to be cool Disney stuff along the way, like photo ops with princesses and pirates. I expected to be sore. I expected there to be lots of hard work training and fundraising.

But.....

I never expected the support of my team over a hundred Jesus-girls, daring to take a stand for a single cause, raising thousands of dollars, one little donation at a time. Complete strangers bonding over a common goal, finally meeting on race weekend, running for those who are not free to run. Yet.

I never expected to be met at the halfway point on Main Street by my precious daughters who got up at 5:30 to ride the monorail to Magic Kingdom just to wave 'Run, Mommy, Run' signs. And yes, I did cry!

I never expected the thousands of volunteers. They were at every mile marker, ready with drinks and water and shouts of encouragement.

I never expected God to whisper so sweetly to me on the long stretches in between. To almost feel His strong hands in the middle of my back pushing me forward.

I never expected to spend so much time encouraging others as we ran. Laughing together, hearing their stories, and helping them go just a little bit further.

I never expected to turn the corner during the last agonizing mile and be met by a gospel choir!

I expected to finish – but I never expected to finish with such joy. To burst into tears when a complete stranger put a finisher medal around my neck! Looking back, maybe it was because it seemed like a tiny taste of what heaven will be like. *"I have fought the good fight. I have kept the faith. There is laid up for me a crown of righteousness which the Lord will give to me on that day.." 2 Timothy 4:7-8 NIV*

And that is what is comes down to, sweet ones. We are all running our race, step by step. Sometimes in the company of many. Sometimes in the agony of alone. But we know that we are running to a goal that is unbelievable.

I pray you can run your race with joy today. That even though life has placed you on a course you never expected, that you can keep taking the next step. May you feel His hand in the middle of your back urging you forward. May you find opportunity to reach out to someone else, even in the middle of your own race. And while your keep your eyes on the prize that is ahead, don't forget to look for the *unexpected* surprises and encouragement He will place in front of you this day.

*Lord, thank You for the unexpected joys You place on my path. Help me be mindful of them and to actively look for You in the midst of the mundane. May You fill me with joy in the "race" of life, one step at a time. Amen*

## April 26

## Asking for Help

By Nancy Howell
*Help carry one another's burdens,*
*and in this way you will obey the law of Christ.*
*Galatians 6:2 GNT*

My late husband and I were a great team. Together we could accomplish most any task. Over the course of a quarter century of life and love together, we became a finely tuned machine.

With two sons, we used the "divide and conquer" mentality--he would take one to various commitments while I handled the other. It worked wonderfully.

That is, until I didn't have him around anymore. He went on up to heaven ahead of me, almost three years ago. The struggle to get simple tasks accomplished after his death is ongoing.

You see, I don't like to ask for help. Well, maybe I should clarify that statement. I don't like to ask *other people* for help.

I have no problem whatsoever asking God. I am thankful for an ever-patient, ever-present Father Who never tires of my asking, because I have done more than my fair share over these past thirty some-odd months.

And even though dear friends want to help my boys and me, I feel like I'm burdening them in the few instances I've actually taken them up on their offers.

Rely on family members? Not an option for us. Our biological families are spread out over Oregon, Kansas, Kentucky, and Massachusetts, while we reside in Texas.

This past weekend, the rubber finally met the road. In other words, I didn't have any other options. I had a son playing baseball one hour away and another son who did not for the life of him want to tag along for the umpteenth time.

I mulled over several scenarios in my mind, but none actually made sense--except calling a friend, a dear sister who has stood beside me during my worst days, and continues to be my sounding board and compass.

I caught myself apologizing as I was explaining my plight over the phone. Before I even got the opportunity to ask for the favor, my friend was agreeing to help me. I hung up the phone feeling relieved, thankful, and happy. I could go along with my baseball-playing son guilt-free, while my younger son was taken care of by beloved friends.

Then I begin to cry. It came out of nowhere, heavy sobs, big tears dripping off of my jaw line.

Not just a few tears, but a full-on ugly cry. The kind of cry where mascara runs as much as your nose. And the nose turns blotchy red in response. I realized in that moment that I cannot do this mom thing alone.

As much as I try, and as much as I plan, there will be times when I am not enough.

My friends, my Christian family, are here for us. We are to "bear one another's burdens"...it is the law of our Savior. They want to be Christ's hands, heart, and feet for me. And my boys and I will be the same for them whenever they are in need.

Whether it's babysitting in a pinch, driving me to and from an upcoming medical appointment, sitting in the stands cheering my baseball-playing son on, or coming to my other son's piano recital, my dear family of God is here for me.

Dear Sisters, in this journey of widowhood, you can only do so much. Outward appearances of having it all together may simply be a mask, covering the self-doubt and sometimes paralyzing fear that we feel, as we traverse through life without the one person who completed us.

All you have to do is ask.

*Dear gracious Father, thank You for amazing Christian friends who are here for me through the good times and the not-so-good times. Give me a willing heart, one that is not too proud to ask for help whenever I most need it. Remind me we are all called to help carry each other's burdens. It is my prayer that You may be glorified through my life. In Jesus' name I ask it all, Amen.*

## April 27

## The Curtain is Torn

By Sheryl Pepple

*And when Jesus had cried out again in a loud voice,*
*he gave up his spirit. At that moment,*
*the curtain of the temple was torn in two from top to bottom.*
*The earth shook and the rocks split.*
*The tombs broke open and the bodies of many holy people*
*who had died were raised to life.*

*Matthew 27:50-53 NIV*

I must confess... some days I want to give up. It is hard to miss my husband so much every day, but particularly around the holidays. Those special days will never quite be the joyous celebration they used to be. We were so caught up in the hustle and bustle of the holidays, temporarily forgetting our troubles and worries as we rushed around with parties and gift buying. It was so much fun to start a New Year, dream about what was to come and plan the vacations we would take. It was as if we had separated ourselves from the world and anything bad by putting up a curtain. And then, in the blink of an eye, my husband was gone, killed by a drunk driver. The "curtain" was torn forever. It is no longer possible to forget about the bad things. I live every day with the knowledge death can intrude in an instant. I live with the pain of missing my husband and the way our life once was. The curtain has been torn - things will never be the same.

Thankfully, I am reminded of another curtain that has been torn - the one at the temple. It was torn the moment Jesus gave up His spirit on the Cross. Prior to that moment, the curtain at the temple separated us from the Most Holy. And then, because of God's grace, it was torn, from the top to the bottom, reconciling us with Him, once and forever.

Because of that torn curtain, we are never alone. God is with us! He is with us on those days we can't get out of bed. He is with us when we look at that empty chair at the table. He is with us when those tears come –yet again. He loves us so much, He allowed His Son to die on the Cross. How precious are we that He would pay such a price. We cannot take the pain of the death of a loved one lightly. We know only too well the cost. Because of that torn curtain, I know without a doubt, He loves me. It changes everything.

I have to let that soak in, again and again – He loves me. He created me. Nothing I can do will ever change His love for me. He cares about each tear I shed. He cares about each step I take. He has a purpose for my life -even now - when I feel so broken. Maybe it is especially now – when I am so broken.

As I continue healing, I see that the curtain that we put up to separate us from suffering can also separate us from God. Because *it is in our suffering*, we cry out to Him, walk with Him, and eventually become more like Him.

Dear Sisters, celebrate today that the curtain has been torn. It changes everything. Don't give up. He loves you. Walk with Him!

## April 28

## Missing Pieces

By Kit Hinkle

*He has shown kindness by giving you rain
from heaven and crops in their seasons;
He provides you with plenty of food
and fills your hearts with joy.*

*Acts 14:17 ESV*

This is what Paul said to the crowd in the Lycaonian city of Lystra when the crowd wanted so badly to have their needs met *their* way, with mythical gods like Zeus and Hermes, instead of getting filled with the *true* God.

Sometimes I do this. I know intellectually that God fills all my emotional needs, but sometimes I still want *what I want my way.* For seven years I have gone without a husband—without arms to hold me at night or someone to handle the pieces of life a man usually handles or just plain being my compass when I feel out of sorts.

Our children do the same thing. Yesterday I spoke with a male friend who has been widowed for several years. As a single father of boys, he asked me, "Kit, do your teenagers cook for themselves sometimes?" I laughed. It's getting better as they get older, but it used to be that I ran all day long, just to keep up with four boys—the idea of a home-cooked meal *by me* sometimes felt foreign. I do cook, but not every night. The boys have gotten quite good at throwing together a salad or heating something up.

My friend hesitated. "And they're good with that?"

I felt guilty for a moment, but then remembered how content my boys are—no complaints about food. "Well, they make a big deal about it when I *do* cook, but they don't complain when I *don't*," I said.

My friend told me his son gets upset when dinner isn't prepared for him.

I thought about how it made so much sense. His son lost a mother. My children didn't. My children don't miss the nurturing side of parenting. But they do complain about the male side of things. One son loves to fish or camp. And I don't have a fishy bone in my body! I tried fishing with him once. The only fun we came away with was laughing at how inept I was at it!

Truth is, for my friend's son who lost a mother, or for my son who lost a father, or for me who lost a husband, **we're all looking for the missing pieces.**

When I notice one of those pieces missing, I sometimes run to my own devices to fix it. I ask my friends to help, and sometimes they can.

But sometimes they can't, and then where do I go? If I'm wise, I turn to prayer and surrender.

Walking the path of widowhood is like being picked up every morning by a gigantic invisible hand, as though I'm one of those tiny people in *Gulliver's Travels*, and being gently plopped on the ground at the foot of the cross. Few other trials in life are so long lasting. It's there with you for years to come, with all the implications of having to brace life alone, hitting you every day.

Sisters, learn to turn to Him sooner. Teach your children to turn to prayer and surrender too. Teach them to be real about their loss. Don't try to jump to fix it all for them, and don't jump to try to fix your own missing pieces. Sometimes just being real that it's tough is the first step in turning to God to fill in those missing pieces.

My prayers for blessings to you as you go into another day and month with your Husband and Father God.

## April 29

### Silence

By Danita Hiles

Silence....

There have been times in my life when it felt like God was simply everywhere. Every time I picked up my Bible, the Word jumped out at me. My prayer life was vibrant and active – I'm talking and He's listening, and He's talking and I'm listening. Every time I turn on the radio, the perfect song playing, and I'm instantly in tears. Daily devotional? Yep, right on the money.

And then there are times like the past few weeks. Times when I pick up my Bible to read, and in the middle of my reading, my mind has wondered to my grocery list. Times when I hear a song on the radio, know it is a great worship opportunity, but I just don't have it in me. Times when I sit in front of the computer and hope for an encouraging e-mail, only to find only a pile of spam messages and solicitations for donations. Times when I am living the Psalmist's words in Psalm 63 NIV – *God, You are my God, earnestly I seek you, my soul thirsts for You, my body longs for You, in a dry and weary land where there is no water…*

At times like this, the silence is deafening.

The lonely is overwhelming.

Last week in the midst of this season of silence, I decided to go running. Laced up my shoes and turned on my music. Now, keep in mind, I am not a RUNNER, I am more of a "poser", slowly trying to work my way up to three miles without collapsing. I decided to put my music on "shuffle" to see what came up. The first song was awesome! The second song, okay, now I was up to a mile and feeling great.

"Thank you, Lord, for this day and this moment," I thought, "I know Lord, that You are going to put the perfect song on next to finish this next long stretch."

I waited- and …..nothing. The silence was deafening. No new song came on. Absolutely nothing was coming from my device. And all I could hear was the sound of my footsteps and my ragged intake of breath. Determined to finish my two miles, I kept plodding on. Step by step. Breath by breath. And with each huff of breath came these words….

God, where…are….You? God, where… are… You?

As I looked up to the heavens, there was no audible answer, but I felt His words replace my question with every step:

*I…am…with…you! I…am…with…you!*

Even in the silence. Even on grey days. Even when I feel empty and hear nothing, He is with me.

Back to Psalm 63- the psalmist goes on to say: *I have seen You in the sanctuary and I beheld Your power and Your glory. Because Your love is better than life,*

Regardless of what you are feeling today – His promises are true.

You see, His presence is not dependent our feelings. It is simply a fact.

I pray that whether you are in an amazing season of revelation or an agonizing season of silence, you will hear His gentle whisper…. *I am with you.*

Oh, and about my two mile run? I made it three miles that day, silence streaming from my device, saying *He is with me*, every step of the way!


# April 30

## Blessing

By Karen Emberlin

*I will make them and the places all around My hill a blessing; and I will cause showers to come down in their season; there shall be showers of blessing.*
*Ezekiel 34:26 NKJV*

A few days ago, I read these words in a devotional: *abundance, cup running over with blessings, uphill, lush meadows, warm sunshine, ease and refreshment*

My very first reaction was, "this is for someone else, not me"! I have been plodding *uphill* for nearly two years now, and even though I feel I have made some progress, it doesn't feel like being in a *lush meadow* drenched with *warm sunshine*! At the end of each day, I feel as though I am still on this journey I did not ask for, and long for the love and companionship of my husband.

I can think of so many things that do not feel like blessings--my husband's unexpected journey to heaven, leaving our home and friends to move hundreds of miles **twice** in the first year, giving up most of our "earthly" possessions, dealing with some serious health issues, and many more.

However, as I began to re-read the words, I began to realize just how "blessed" I am. Many of the things I have experienced on this journey are really blessings in disguise. They have come through tears and pain, but have caused me to draw closer to the Lord, depending only on Him.

Because of the distance I needed to move and the uncertainty of my future, it was necessary to give up most of our "earthly possessions". All of the stuff we had collected over forty-eight years suddenly became a burden! It was not easy to give up some things, but a blessing in the long run, especially for the second move.

I am so thankful for my children. My first move allowed me to spend time with my daughter and her family. What a blessing to be with my grandchildren and get to know them better. Even though my son is many miles away, he calls me every day to make sure I am okay - a blessing only a Mom can understand.

In spite of the loss of my husband and the loneliness I still feel, my cup **is** running over with many blessings!

I believe that perhaps the *"lush meadow"* drenched in *warm sunshine* is now where I call "home". My second move took me back to the community where I was born and raised - a special blessing to be back with my mom, other family members, and friends after being gone for nearly forty years. In this season of my life, I needed a place where I could feel safe and secure, a place to be able to heal, and to grow in the Lord. I not only "receive" many blessings each day, but have many opportunities to give and "share" God's love with others. It is not only what we *receive* but what we *give* that allows us to heal!

My life today is not "my choice" – I would choose to be sharing it with my husband, but God's choice for me is different. I will never forget the love my husband and I shared for forty-eight years, however, God is blessing me with ways to share and heal in this season of my life.

I pray that you will take time to reflect on the "blessings" God has given to you on this "unwanted journey". It may not be the one you have asked for, but **the journey that takes you closer to God is so worth the trip**!

# MAY

## May 1

### Super-storm

By Erika Graham

*Though he slay me, yet will I trust in him...*
*Job 13:15 NIV*

Hurricane Sandy hit the East Coast in 2012 and my little area of the world was turned upside down. The town bordering mine, where many of my friends and family call home, looked like someone had taken the majority of it, thrown it in a blender, added lots of sand and water, ran it on high, then dumped it back out.

It was utter and complete devastation!

Afterwards, the world seemed to descend on us with help, as we rallied around each other, and slowly the needs of those affected were met. Everyone banded together, and it was an amazing blessing to witness. Yet, almost two years later, some are still trying to recover in one way or another.

Throughout, I've felt a strange but strong connection to it all, I guess because I could relate to being a "super-storm survivor". After all, I had suffered through and survived my own, a few years earlier. When my husband died so suddenly, I was in a super-storm, where my life had been thrown into a blender and dumped back out. I felt the utter devastation and had to endure the "unending" mess.

I was blessed to have a "disaster relief team" too, composed of an amazing inner circle of family and friends who came in and met all our earthly needs. The kids and I felt lost, sad, and hopeless at times. We became frustrated and angry too, just like the Sandy victims. Our recovery process was slow and often took unexpected turns, as well.

At the time Sandy had hit, God prompted me to study the book of Job, a portrayal of how God allows a good man to suffer. Job was a materially and spiritually blessed man of God, who stood out (Job 1:1). Even God himself is well pleased with this man (Job 1:8). But, God allows Satan to strip Job of everything; his family, his possessions, his land, and his health. Job is stricken with intense grief over the multitude of losses. He winds up asking the question we all have, "Why me?" That's when God proves His power and sovereignty by appearing to Job in a storm, of all things.

What presses on me about this story is that everyone around him wanted him to blame God and turn from Him, even his wife. Job had no "disaster relief team" to help during this super-storm. He was in it all alone, and those around were trying hard to pull him down. Yet, Job knew his God, his only "disaster relief" team, was all he needed.

But, Job grieved, he lamented, he cried out, he pleaded, and he even wrestled with and questioned God. In the end, God sent a clear message that He IS in control and Job yielded to His power and authority. Even when he was greatly tempted to blame God and turn from Him, his faith remained and he proclaimed, "I know that You can do all things; no plan of Yours can be thwarted" Job 42:2.

Then, Job was rewarded with even greater blessings than he had before.

Friends, losing your husband can put you in a super-storm, and the devastation and aftermath is forever imprinted on your lives. Like Job, you might feel all alone in this journey, or like me you might be blessed to have a "disaster relief team" of friends and family to come around you.

Either way, I encourage you to remember that we do have a supernatural "team" Who is here for us; Our God, Our Jesus, and the Holy Spirit dwelling within us. And we can look to this Team to minister to us and to alone see us through.

*Heavenly Father, help me look to You in the midst of this storm. Help me trust You and seek You. Thank You for guiding me and strengthening me in each and every moment. In Your Matchless Name, Amen.*

## May 2

## Troubled Church

By Kit Hinkle

*Fearing people is a dangerous trap,*
*but trusting the LORD means safety.*

*Proverbs 29:25 NLT*

Have you ever visited a home where a certain room was off-limits and never entered? It feels a bit creepy to me. I believe every room needs to be enjoyed and lit up with noise and activity, or else it's a house—not a home.

There was a specific church, that for a while, I felt my boys and I weren't allowed to go. It had undergone a horrible rift. And though I wasn't part of the rift—and I refused to choose sides— my family loved and was mentored so sweetly by the pastor and his wife. We left our old church and joined them at their new church.

So you can bet it was difficult when, two years later, circumstances changed once more. That pastor and his family got called away to another mission. I found myself looking, yet again, for a church home in which to get my boys settled.

I visited our former church, full of beautiful sisters and brothers who welcomed us back after being away two years. We received hug after genuine hug, some from ladies who came running and whooping toward us to clutch us in their arms.

"My son spotted you and I told him, 'Stop her before she leaves. I've just got to hug her!!!'"

I was overwhelmed by our red carpet reception, but was at odds within my heart. How could people so loving and kind have hurt precious friends of our family? I keenly felt love for these brothers and sisters, but also anger over a compromised body of Christ. The painful memories of the struggle between them contrasted with my desire for my boys to rekindle old friendships.

The new pastor at the church spoke about forgiveness and taking your time to respond to people who have hurt you, rather than quickly retaliating. You can do the Christian thing and turn the other cheek, but still feel the anger stinging in your heart. "We have a responsibility to forgive," he said.

**Forgive.** *I think I've done that.*

**Love these people.** *There's no doubt I do. I've known them for years, and I know they care a great deal for me.*

**Be loyal to friends.** *I've certainly stood by the pastor and his family through their difficult years.*

So why was I unsettled about revisiting the old church and its congregation?

Late one night, way after my twelve-year-old's bedtime, he knocked on my door. "Mom, I found a Bible verse in my reading that might help you."

Words from the mouths of babes. It was a Bible verse about fear. The Bible is filled with God's instruction not to fear. Proverbs 29:25 says, *"Fearing people is a dangerous trap, but trusting the LORD means safety".*

Once my son woke me up to what was gnawing at me—fear—I was able to tackle it and turn it over to the Lord. Then I had the freedom to choose a church based on our family's needs, not the needs of another family.

In the end, we decided to attend a different church. I located an amazing youth program run by a pastor who truly loves my boys and welcomed them into his fold instantly.

God brought me back to our old church to shine a light on and expose a fear. But I don't feel any obligation to attend or NOT attend that church based on my friends' needs or expectations. The Lord freed me from the fear of hurting anyone's feelings and placed my boys and me in just the right church community for this season of our lives.

*Father God, help me strive to stay connected to a church community, to choose one based on Your Word, and not to shy away from any body of Christ over fear. It's You whom we worship at church, not the sense of belonging or the correctness of how a church is operating. In Christ's name, Amen.*

## May 3

## Don't Leave Home Without It

By Elizabeth Dyer


I left the house naked recently.

Now, before you call the police on me, let me explain. I left the house naked of my spiritual "clothes".

Have you ever done this?

We rush out the door consumed with the day's agenda, without giving a thought to our spiritual health. It happens once, twice, three times, and by then it becomes forgotten.

It has always been a challenge for me to find time to spend in God's Word. But this school year, God has provided time in my day for putting on my spiritual "clothes". There is a twenty minute lull in the morning between some kids leaving and some kids waking so I have just enough time to sit down with my flavored coffee and read my One Year Bible.

How about you? Do you have a set time to sit with God? This happens to be my routine this year. Yours may and probably will look completely different. I encourage you to pray about finding time in your daily routine for spiritual growth.

On the topic of spiritual "clothes", I looked up how many verses talk about putting on or putting off. The Apostle Paul talked about it several times in his letters to the churches in the New Testament. (all verses NIV) Here are just a few:

- Ephesians 4:24 "and to **put on** the new self, created to be like God in true righteousness and holiness."

- Ephesians 6:11 "**Put on** the full armor of God, so that you can take your stand against the devil's schemes."
- 1 Thessalonians 5:8 "But since we belong to the day, let us be sober, **putting on** faith and love as a breastplate, and the hope of salvation as a helmet."

And then there are verses on clothing yourselves. Just to get you started...

- Colossians 3:12-13 "Therefore, as God's chosen people, holy and dearly loved, **clothe** yourselves with compassion, kindness, humility, gentleness and patience... And over all these virtues **put on** love, which binds them all together in perfect unity."
- I Peter 5:5 "All of you, **clothe** yourselves with humility toward one another..."

**Choose one from the list of things to put on or clothe yourself with** each day before you walk out of your bathroom. This is one way to hide God's Word in your heart. Why do we need to do that? *Psalm 119:11 (NIV) I have hidden your word in my heart that I might not sin against you.*

I think I am going to choose gentleness for the first week. Will you join me?

Let's set the standard in our families and allow them to see us putting on these qualities and becoming more Christ-like. Only YOU can prevent Spiritual Nakedness...

*Lord God, show me exactly when we can spend time together. I really want to keep growing. I want to set my sights higher than just surviving. Show me, guide me, lead me so I don't leave home without my spiritual clothing. Amen*

## <u>May 4</u>

## It Will Turn Out Okay

By Karen Emberlin

*I have told you all this so that you may have peace in me.*
*Here on earth you will have many trials and sorrows.*
*But take heart, because I have overcome the world.*

*John 16:33 NLT*

Certain times of the year seem to be filled with so many things to accomplish. There are parties to give and others to attend, shopping to do, scheduling of holiday time with family, travel plans, and so much more. Whew!! Tension builds and on many days my "widow" brain just can't handle all of it!

So, when I just want to forget it all and try to relax I find myself clicking through the channels to find one of "those" movies! I am sure you all know what I am talking about. The ones that run back to back every night and all week-end long. Ones you don't mind seeing only once, but maybe even two or three times!

I find I can get very wrapped up in the stories and can experience all the emotions from laughter to tears. I may be looking for simple entertainment, but I find these movies also offer an escape – an escape from reality and a way to release my own emotions! A chance to let the tears flow and hide the real reason. Even though I can relate to many of them, the stories that are portrayed are not "real" but "make believe". They may contain some of the struggles of life, but you can be sure they will "always" turn out OK and have a "happy ending"!

The last evening my husband and I watched
TV together, I tuned in to one of "those" movies after
he had watched some of his favorite programs. With
almost half of it to go, and of course the most
important half, he decided to go on to bed. His
comment was, "You can stay up and watch the rest of
the movie – but I can already tell you, it will turn out
okay."

The movie that night did have a happy ending
and it did turn out okay. However, the next morning
when I woke to find that my husband had made his
unexpected journey to heaven in his sleep, I was sure
"our" story did not turn out okay! In the many years
we shared together, we experienced the ups and downs
of life, so, as we approached our "golden years", why
couldn't our story have a "happy" ending like all those
movies?!

If I really believe (and I do) the movies are
"make believe" then I must dismiss those thoughts
from my mind and replace them with the "truth" from
God's word. He tells us in John 16:33 there will be
troubles in this world, but that they are temporary and
are preparing us for an eternal glory. **Our peace is not
in the absence of strife or troubles, but in Jesus
and what He has done to make our future sure**!

Even though our story may not be as I wanted,
it does have a happy ending. I know my husband no
longer has to face the trials and struggles of this life on
Earth. I know he is in Heaven with our Lord and
Savior, and I will join him one day.

I may not know when my part of our "story"
on earth will be complete. I know there will continue
to be trials as long as I am here, but I know He is

preparing a place for me in Heaven and He will take care of me until He calls me home.

*Lord, I know the trials experienced here on Earth are only temporary. I pray for the peace only you can give, a peace that passes all understanding. Help me put my trust in You alone. Amen*

## May 5

## Moving Toward or Away?

By Teri Cox

> *But he said to me, "My grace is sufficient for you,*
> *for my power is made perfect in weakness."*
> *Therefore I will boast all the more gladly of my weaknesses,*
> *so that the power of Christ may rest upon me.*
> *2 Corinthians 12:9 ESV*

I have been in the process of moving. I now remember why I don't like moving; **it is hard**. Hard, to pack everything, hard to decide what stays and what goes, hard to decide what should be thrown away and what should be kept, hard work, hard days with long hours. It's just hard. Not only is moving physically difficult, but it's emotionally taxing.

However, as I get closer and closer to a new home and a fresh start, I grow more and more hopeful for what God has next. Where will He take me? What will He ask of me? Will there be new adventures, new loves, new interests, or new beginnings?

I wonder if the disciples ever woke up wondering what was next.

"What will Jesus do today?"

"Where will He take us?"

"Will we see a miracle today?"

"How big will the crowds get?"

I love the fact that God's Word is not just full of their perfect stories and their great moments, but also of their missteps and less than perfect decisions. Peter's triumphs and epic failures are out there for us to see. He walked on water, and then took his eyes off the master and began to sink. He loved Jesus full-out, and yet denied ever knowing Him.

Thomas was chosen and yet he did not believe until he had proof he could touch with his own hands. There were squabbles among them; about who loved Jesus more and whom He loved the most. Pride and arrogance got the best of them too, even though they walked, literally walked, with The Master.

Paul cried out from his knees, in sickness, for God to remove his afflictions. God said no, and Paul accepted that it was best. He learned how to be content in pain, in prison, in all things. (2 Corinthians 12:10)

It has brought me to the question, am I content? I must admit, I had a bit of a meltdown the other day, after my hardwood floors, from 1947, had been restored. They are breathtaking, beautiful, and ready to be lived on, but it is not me that gets to enjoy them for years to come. Am I content with that? At the moment, I was not but now, now I am. They will be a wonderful setting for the next family God has for this home. I pray that it will be as welcoming for them as it was for us. My husband, Daryl, told me when we were looking for this house, "It will be our perfect house, given to us in God's perfect timing." He was right, as usual. It was perfect for us and now it will be perfect

151

for someone else. So, as I look forward, what "perfect" thing will God have for me now, in my new tiny house with my precious friends so close by? I'm not sure yet, but I'm moving toward it.

*God, give me peace and excitement for all the days You still have for me here. I long to know that You have not forgotten me and that Your dream for my life is not complete. Help me to live it, love it, and move toward it. Amen*

## May 6

## Because We Are All Life-givers

By Kit Hinkle

> *The LORD your God is in your midst,*
> *a mighty one who will save;*
> *he will rejoice over you with gladness;*
> *he will quiet you by his love;*
> *he will exult over you with loud singing.*
>
> *Zephaniah 3:17 ESV*

With Mother's Day coming, I want to dedicate this post to three types of mothers:

1. **the weary and cheery**: those who are raising or caring for their kids right now by themselves without a husband
2. **the matriarch**: those whose kids have flown away and are facing widowhood without kids in the house, and
3. **all other life-givers**: those who I'd like to recognize their unique ways of offering motherhood to this world.

**To the weary, but cheery:**

Let your children bless you. Relax and embrace your kids as they embrace you.

My kids do breakfast in bed. It's usually some kind of burnt toast, but over the years it's getting better. Then we head out to an outdoor cafe after church. The best part? It's their way of celebrating-not mine.

I know that sounds odd, but for me, I'd rather have handmade cards from their hearts than a list of things I ask them to get for me.

**To the Matriarch:**

Since I'm still in the trenches of raising kids, I can sometimes think to myself, "Empty-nester – what a choice place to be as a widow!" But who knows how I'll feel when the last one leaves – thrilled? happy? lost? lonely? having regrets? Quiet all these thoughts, Sister, as you just bask in this day of adoration for mothers. For no matter what the situation, you have done it! May today give you the feeling of the Lord singing to you, like a bird answering you in your empty nest, of our verse from Zephaniah.

**To the Life-giver:**

Perhaps you wanted more children or perhaps you and your husband never had kids. Either way, Mother's Day can have a particularly painful tone to it.

A dear friend who could never have children called me when she turned forty. She and her husband have struggled with multiple disabilities. Between all the medical complications, it was time to admit their womb would be closed forever. But another call later, she shared with me from Matthew twenty. Jesus tells us the parable about the workers in the field. The master hired some workers early in the day and some late in the day, but paid them the same—valued them the same. **Whether He gives one of the job of ten kids, another the job of one kid, or still another, no kids, He still values each of us as mothers and life-givers according to His plan.**

God wired all of us for life-giving. Sisters, let's pray for each other on Mother's Day.

*Dear Father God, please remind me as I do Mother's Day without my earthly husband of what life-givers I am. Please step in and remind me of my value and worth to You and Your kingdom. Amen.*

## May 7

## Who He Says I Am

By Lori Reynolds Streller

My eyes flutter open. It is a rare day when no
alarm clock is needed and the morning calendar is void
of events. A few months into the newness of
widowhood, I lie in bed realizing that I am different.

I ask myself, "Who am I now?"

I'm one of those old-fashioned girls who
always wanted to be a wife and mother. There is no
shame in that. I enjoyed my career too, but role of wife
and mother was my dream "job". I thrived being under
the loving leadership of my husband.

He is gone now.

It is clear *who I am not*. I was my husband's
primary caregiver during his cancer battle. Suddenly, I
am no longer the charter and giver of all medications,
the guider of his walker as he navigates his way out of
his home hospital bed, no longer the overseer of
changing his clothing, the administer of nourishment
through his feeding tube, no longer the helper for his
personal care, nor the one reading to him as his eyes
fail.

As I stretch my memory past the illness, to the
beautiful years of our marriage, I find that I have lost
many other pieces of myself as well. I am without my
best-friend, the Spiritual leader of our home, my
parenting partner, my lover, and my biggest fan. *(Wow.
That's a huge loss in one single blink of an eye.)*

Thankfully, I am still Mom to our two children.
But even that role has changed. I have new
responsibilities as the only parent in this home. I am
the sole overseer of homework, sports schedules,

chores, and nutrition. I am the lone chauffeur for all road trips, long or short. I am the one to guide our children, emotionally and physically, as they navigate grief and the early teen years.

To be honest, it's a lot, but you already know this, because you too are walking the lonely road of the widow. Some of you are also raising children during this transition. Whether we have that common thread or not, I am guessing you feel like you've lost a chunk of who you are also.

So much has changed. WHO are we now?

I have a rule that I have implemented in my life to keep my train of thought positive when life is topsy-turvy.

**When you are unsure of something, go back to what you KNOW is true.**

So, what is true about who we are?

We are children of the most high God (Acts 17:28).

We are forever His treasured possession (Deuteronomy 7:6).

We are guided by Truth (John 16:13).

We are forgiven (Ephesians 1:7).

We are fully complete, strengthened in His might, lacking nothing (Colossians 1:11 and 2:10).

We are holy and dearly loved (Colossians 3:12).

Losing the role of wife has shaken me to my core. It has left me feeling lonely, awkward and lost. Can you relate? I am so thankful that God reminds us of our worth, regardless of what our earthly "titles" are. **We are still precious and beautiful in His sight.** He wants us to see the beauty that remains within us. Let's rest in the knowledge of *who He says we are*!

*Lord, thank You for staying with me right in the messy middle of my life (Hebrews 13:5b). This life gets ugly, and it is so easy to lose sight of my true identity. You call me "loved", "accepted", and "friend". Wow. Remind me when I forget, Lord. Let me feel the saturation of who You say I am from the inside out. Amen.*

## May 8

## Whithersoever I Go

By Sherry Rickard

*Have I not commanded thee?*
*Be strong and of a good courage;*
*be not afraid, neither be thou dismayed;*
*for the Lord thy God is with thee whithersoever thou goest.*
*Joshua 1:9 KJV*

The grief journey is a lonely journey, and one you have to travel yourself - no one can do it for you. It takes a lot of intentional work and an earnest heart that is focused on healing, surviving, and thriving. You must be focused on your Savior - **eyes up**, looking to the Savior; **ears open**, listening to the Savior's voice; **feet walking** on the path set out. These must be done day in and day out.

I am now coming up to the four year anniversary of my husband's Homecoming, or Promotion, as I like to call it. Four years since I last kissed my husband's lips. When I look back, it doesn't seem possible I am here at this spot in the road.

*Where* am I? *Who* am I?

If I take note of where I've been and who I've met along the way, it is clear that I am an abundantly blessed woman. Clearly, I am favored in God's eyes.

157

He has been with me "whithersoever" I have been and for that I am grateful.

During this journey I have hidden from Him, not spoken to Him, cried out to Him, longed for His return, and beseeched Him. I have loved Him, understood His answer to my prayers about my husband's life, forgiven Him, renewed my relationship with Him, and felt His presence.

I have met some wonderful people along the way who have been like life-preservers thrown in the water to a drowning person. God sent them to me to help me to look up to Him. I have been on trips and tours that I would have never taken. I have laughed really hard. I have met widow-sisters who know my thoughts. God knew I needed them.

Most of all, I have come to realize that God has a purpose for me. He has a ministry for me, and He has grown or is growing all of the unique skills and tools I need to accept His calling.

As I look back down the road I have travelled so far, the constant that I see along every stretch of the road, around every bend, in every valley and on every mountaintop, is Christ. He has never left me. I may have walked ahead or stayed behind, but my Savior was there the whole time. He has had His eye on me; working with me, on me - sending me people, resources, experiences that just strengthen my roots in Him.

I don't know what God has in store for me, but I know He has a purpose for me--He will be with me every step of the way. I just have to be strong and of good courage and not let fear limit my ability to be obedient to Him.

*Dear Lord, thank You for never leaving me and for going wherever I go. Thank You for loving me and for providing me with experiences that grow me into the person You need me to be. I love You! Amen*


## May 9

### You Don't Have to Forget to Re-set!

By Kit Hinkle

Ever feel like it's hard to hit the reset button on your life because it means you must forget what's behind you? Don't believe that! When Paul talks about forgetting what lies behind in Philippians, he doesn't mean forgetting the good things from our past. Here is Paul's statement in *Philippians 3:13b*: *"But one thing I do: forgetting what lies behind and straining forward to what lies ahead."*

Often, remembering the wonderful things about marriage and God's goodness in the past increases our hope for the future ... especially when we're ready to date again.

As a boost to his dreary situation, the Psalmist wrote, *"I will remember the deeds of the Lord; yes, I will remember your wonders of old"* (Psalm 77:11). Recounting God's faithfulness in uniting my husband Tom and me is a reminder He can do that for me again. Now, if I get remarried that doesn't mean my new husband will have the same attributes or each of the great qualities Tom had. Nor should I expect that or have a sense of entitlement to that goodness as I date.

I think of entrepreneurs who successfully build a business, only to have something totally out of their control destroy it—a bad economy, a hurricane, or an embezzling employee. They lost what seems to be "it all". And, in order for those entrepreneurs to build a new business, they need to let go of how unfair their loss feels. They need to be ready to start over with new goals. Remembering the good times in the past can help give them courage and hope for a fresh beginning, even though it won't be the same as before. They may have a new storefront, employees, or even products/services they offer.

I want to compare that process of starting over to a widow's process of starting over, but then, yes. I know. It's different with the love of your life; I know that because I've been there.

I remember that transformation taking place for me. In those early years after losing Tom, I had no interest in moving forward with dating. I still felt married in my heart—just having to do all the work of raising the kids alone.

It was a few years out when my younger boys asked me to start dating. That's when I recognized a longing for companionship; I was ready to begin starting over. I approached my first few dating experiences wanting to see lightning strike again—like it had with Tom. What a difficult standard to set for men in my path!

But then I began to see these new friendships along the dating road as unique and different. I began to see my life as unique and different like aNew Season where I can explore what type of person fits my future. I realized I still appreciated who Tom had been and the many amazing things about our marriage. But I didn't expect a replica of him or our good times in a new relationship. No, now I was considering a different type of person in my future.

You may not be ready to date yet … or ever. And that's okay. Or maybe you do feel like it's time. Either way, take hope in God's past goodness as a sign of His faithfulness for your future. Remembering all the wonderful things about my marriage and Tom gives me plenty of hope. If the Lord wills for me to marry again, I'll love my new husband—unique qualities and all!

*Father God, I need to forget my sense of unfairness (over losing my husband) in order to move forward. Would You help me see Your goodness through that process? Please encourage me through Your Holy Spirit that Your love is present even when I'm expressing anger. Give me rest from the fight. Calm my heart and give me a new outlook. Like a teenager ready to begin anew—alone in the world, but not alone—I have You! I pray this in Your Precious Son's Name, Amen*

## May 10

## God is Good, Even When It Seems Bad Part 1

By Sherry Rickard and Elizabeth Dyer

*And we know that in all things God works
for the good of those who love Him,
who have been called according to His purpose.*

*Romans 8:28 NIV*

Everywhere you turn; it seems there is a sad story...in our lives, on the news, in our schools, churches, at work, everywhere. As Christians, we turn what the world "worries" about, over to Christ, and we do that through prayer.

What happens when you pray earnestly, with proper intentions, and God's answer is not what you prayed for? What happens when your worst fears are not taken away, but realized? God may be asking you, or someone you love, to bear pain that seems unbearable, unthinkable, un-survive-able.

*Is God still good during these times? Is He still there? Does He know what He is asking of us? Does He care?*

What do you do when God's answer is, "No, my child."? Or, "Not yet, my child."? Or, "Yes, darling child, but not as you imagined it would be." The writing team felt called to share with you where we stand regarding the statement, "God is good - even when it seems bad", in the hope you would be encouraged.

*~Sherry Rickard*

**Elizabeth Dyer** *:* There was a time in my life when so much was going "wrong" that I felt like God had dumped a truck load of manure on my head. It was

BIG stuff going "wrong" – marriage issues, job loss, declining health, letting go of my children's education. Prayers are unanswered. Peace could not be found. Pain grew with each breath. How was it that I was supposed to believe God was **still** good?

My faith was shaken to its very foundation. I finally came face-to-face with Scripture and had a choice to make. Either God was still the God of the Old Testament whose name is Elohim, Strong One, who says to me, "Don't be afraid. I am with you." Either He was the God of the New Testament who silenced the storms and promises to always work our life's events out to His glory. Or He wasn't any of this- He was a fraud and a destroyer. I couldn't accept that He was my enemy so I had to accept the other. I clung to Him as my Creator and Lover of my soul. It was all I had to hang on to.

When I had *only* God to cling to, I changed the focus of my prayers. Previously, my prayers had been really good, but really *mine*. I was convicted to change my prayers to simply, "Not my will, but Yours." I wanted all kinds of great things, but I dropped all that baggage at the foot of the cross. I walked away with only five words. Those five words were proof whether I really did trust God fully with my life.

And that's where I return every time things seem to point to God's not being good. We probably would never put these horrific events in our testimonies but God has chosen to *trust us* with these circumstances so we must *trust Him* with them too.

So do I trust Him or not? That is what it boils down to. Sometimes I fight with myself over the answer. I trust, but... No, that isn't true trust. I have to trust completely. God is good, all the time. All the time, God is good.

*Father God, You are good. You are wise. Give me faith to accept that truth today, through good and bad. I completely trust You with my life. Not my will but Yours. Amen*

## May 11

## God is Good, Even When It Seems Bad, Part 2

By Ami Atkins and Linda Lint

Whenever I'm posed with the question, "How is God good when bad things happen?" I run immediately to the cross where Jesus faced the worst thing.

Yet He was willing to bear the crushing weight of sin, to absorb the fireball of the Father's wrath that should have been hurled at humanity, to be rejected so that we could be accepted.

How could that possibly have been good? How could a good God willingly turn away from His Son? How could the Son also willingly offer His life?

The powers of hell thought they'd won. The one called Messiah hung there dead. God lost. He was not powerful, and apparently, He was not good.

But, oh, my friends don't stop there! The plan was bigger, the goodness of God incomprehensible. On the third day Jesus rose conquering death and hell!

Now don't miss the radical nature of what Jesus accomplished. He purchased salvation. He satisfied God's righteous wrath toward sinful men. He redeemed His own, buying back those who once went a whoring after other gods. While we were His enemies, He died for us.

He is good. It is His very nature. From the heart of the Father, flowed the grand plan of redemption before time began. At the cross it came to fruition. God saved men from Himself. God saved men to Himself.

**Jesus faced the ultimate bad so that we could know the ultimate good.**

Life. Hope. Peace. Grace. Eternity. Reconciliation.

Therefore, if God has already done the ultimate good to me, He will always do good to me. (Romans 8:32). I can count on that!

**Linda Lint:** "God is good - even when it seems bad" is a simple, absolute truth. Our God is always good, always present for us when the "its" of life come barging into our days. The "its" of illness, broken relationships, financial struggles, and death bring us pain and sorrow. Yet, through it all God stands ready with only the comfort He can provide and a sustaining grace to carry us through the trial.

God makes it clear to us in His words to Isaiah, *"My thoughts are not your thoughts, neither are your ways My ways" (Isaiah 55:8)*. And we are told many times throughout the New Testament that we **will** have trials and struggles. We are also given the promise from Jesus Himself in Matthew 28:20, He will never leave you – He is always with you. God knows our pain. He counts every tear that falls when those "its" come. Sometimes He gives us understanding - sometimes He does not.

For me, it is wonderful when God moves in and resolves an "it" in my life. It is also a great comfort for me to know that when one of those "its" does not have a quick easy answer, He is right there alongside me collecting my tears and hearing every word my hurting heart is saying.

When understanding of the negative "its" of life does not readily come, I am learning to "*Trust in the Lord with all my heart and to lean not on my own understanding*". (Proverbs 3:5) When I lean into trusting God, I find a solid support that will sustain me until the day I am with Him in eternity.

*Jesus, I want to trust You today. When I see the evil and sickness around me, it is so easy to take my eyes off the Cross and look at everything else. When I bring my concerns to You, help me trust You to work through them for Your glory. And help me give up my right to answers to all my questions. You are good, all the time. Amen*

## May 12

## God is Good, Even When It Seems Bad, Part 3

By Jill Byard and Katie Oldham

> *Trust in the Lord with all your heart*
> *and lean not on your own understanding;*
> *in all your ways submit to him,*
> *and he will make your paths straight.*
> *Proverbs 3:5-6 NIV*

While reading the Proverbs passage, I catch a glimpse of God's Father-personality so clearly. I see Him and me sitting at the kitchen table having a deep conversation. As I see the conversation starting to wrap up, I stand up and start for the door. As I walk away, He gives me one more piece of advice. He squeezes my hand and recites this verse.

It is not by happenstance that His first directive is to trust His heart and the second is a warning to not be too confident in my head knowledge. See, singing about trusting Him, reading about trusting Him, and listening to teachings about trusting Him, fills up my own understanding and builds confidence in my head knowledge. Head knowledge is important to obtain, but if it stands alone, I become a law keeper. That never ends well.

"When I cannot see His hand, I must trust His heart." When situations arise and etch gaping canyons in my heart, I have to remember He wastes nothing and He sees beyond the now into eternity. He wants the best for His daughter. His heart surrounds me on all sides. He knows the road ahead. He created it. He gave His only Son to make a way for His children. His heart is worthy of my trust. His goodness towards me sustains me like a life raft.

**Katie Oldham:** Since the beginning of time, we see God fulfilling promises and prophesy. He IS sovereign, Sisters! The thing is...our human minds were never meant to grasp His ways and His infinite wisdom. We were meant, on bended knees and with bowed heads, to surrender, to trust and to sing His praises in ALL things. He reveals understanding to us in His perfect time and with His loving care for our ability to handle it or use it in our lives.

So, while we cannot understand His ways, we CAN trust Him fully with assurance that all things from Him are good and born of His unconditional love for us. Just like He fulfilled promises and prophesy during Biblical times, we can trust His purpose for our lives today and use it for His glory. We can rest knowing our lives were created for eternity with Him and He guides us in every step of our earthly journeys until we reach His heavenly presence. So, let us always be encouraged by huddling into His sovereign, capable hand!

*Christ Jesus, today I pray back our verse in Proverbs. I want to trust You with all my heart. Please develop this trust in me today. Help me not lean on my own understanding. I submit everything to You as You make my ways straight. Amen*

## May 13

## God is Good, Even When It Seems Bad, Part 4

By Lori Reynolds Streller and Bonnie Vickers

Trusting in God's goodness, it's what I always seem to come back to when everything flips topsy-turvy and I find myself disoriented and unsure of things in this life. Sometimes it is hard to see goodness around me in the midst of tragedy. It is then that I must trust in the unchanging character of our God. He is all-powerful, all-knowing, and all-sufficient. He is always good, even when it seems bad. Even in death. That's not an easy thing to process when the life of a loved one ends, when pleas for healing seem to go unanswered. But He is *always* good. And you know what else? He always heals His children. *ALWAYS!* The healing may not come on this earth, but our loved ones are healed in the presence of their Savior. And that, my Sisters, is a healing that can never be erased or marred by death again.

*"The Lord is good to all and His tender mercies are over all His work." Psalm 145:9 KJV*

His focus is on the eternal. Cling to His goodness. When life is ripped out from underneath you and you are free falling into a dark abyss, know that He is with you. He never leaves us, He never forsakes us. No matter how dismal this life gets…we win in the end. Because, God is good!

**Bonnie Vickers:**

*He has made everything beautiful in His time.*
*Ecclesiastes 3:11 NKJV*

Even in this journey of grief through widowhood, He will make it beautiful. Jesus will always come between us and our sorrows, our pain, our fears. We cannot get away from God. His goal isn't necessarily to make us happy. His goal is to make us His. Becoming the person God wants you to be takes time. And it doesn't come easily or overnight. And often, it comes at a great cost or loss. It is a process of walking every day with Him; asking Him to pierce our soul. Even in the midst of trials and tribulations, we must allow Him to mold us, shape us, change us and move us.

*God, thank You that my feeling of happiness is not Your ultimate goal in my life! Your goal for me is growth in our relationship. Thank You for Your tender mercies in my life. Give me eyes to see them today. Amen*

## May 14

## God is Good, Even When It Seems Bad, Part 5

By Leah Stirewalt and Teri Cox

I remember that day in 2007 vividly. I had been offered my dream job. I knew God had been preparing me for it. The hiring manager simply asked me to pray about it for a few more days and then call her back to let her know. I agreed to do so, even though I knew I would be accepting the position.

You can imagine my horror when I woke up the next morning and felt unsettled about taking the position. The pay was fine, the benefits were great, and the hours were perfect! What could possibly be causing my hesitation? Two days later, I called the hiring manager back, and by this time I knew. I could not take the job. I was so disappointed that God would allow me to go through the process only to tell me "not yet", but that's what I distinctly felt He was saying to me. I knew I was supposed to work there, but I didn't know when...until 2011.

The same position I had been offered before was open again. I repeated the application process, and on May 3, I was offered the position! This time I accepted it.

*The difference?*

May 3, 2011, was the very day my husband took his life. God knew I would not be able to support my daughter and myself with my previous salary or be able to afford the insurance through my previous employer. God knew things I couldn't possibly know in 2007, and

171

He protected me from something that needed to happen later in my life. His timing and sovereignty are always perfect!

**Teri Cox:** There are moments in this world that drives us to our knees; that take us to the edge of the abyss and threatens to hurl us over. This world is NOT what God intended for us. He created a beautiful, peaceful Garden of Eden for us, not this. This world is broken, fallen, and filled with sin and sorrow. It will *shatter* us into a million pieces and throw us away; counting us useless or finished.

However, as His children, we can be made new, because He is our "potter". *But now, O Lord, You are our Father, We are the clay, and You our potter; And all of us are the work of Your hand* . (Isaiah 64:8 NASB) We may not look like we did before, or function with the same purpose we had before. Yet still, cracked, leaking, mended, or entirely refashioned, **we can be useful and we are loved.**

How do I know, "God is Good-Even When It Seems Bad"? Because, I know God is *just* and sees the tapestry of eternity. When I look at broken circumstances I too become broken. When I look at Him, I become new and He draws *faith* out of me. "Lord, I believe; help me in my unbelief!" (Mark 9:24) Amen

## May 15

### God is Good, Even When It Seems Bad, Part 6

By Erika Graham and Kit Hinkle

*I remain confident of this:*
*I will see the goodness of The Lord in the land of the living.*
*Psalm 27:13 NIV*

As life has unfolded over the last few years, I've pondered this verse often. It sits with me, and it stirs my mind and heart almost daily. It's hard to understand or fathom at times, how this life and the horrific stuff that I see and experience could *possibly* be good or become good. How could God's goodness ever be in some of these terrible circumstances? The suffering, the brokenness, the unfairness, the injustice, and just the messy world around me make it seem bleak at times.

Yet, these are the things I do know: God is Sovereign and is always in control, ever working in our circumstances, walking alongside us, and allowing the good and the bad in life. As I pray and contemplate His goodness, I realize that God's goodness is *not* found in my good or bad circumstances. Focusing on my circumstances would cause me to never see His goodness, unless things were perfect every day and, even then, my flesh would be unsatisfied. Instead, I have learned His goodness is in His love and care for me, His constant presence and provision over me, and His healing power running through me. And mostly, His goodness is in Jesus Christ.

I am loved, cared for, and forgiven through Christ. I can experience that goodness every day, even if that day is the most gut wrenching, difficult day I've ever experienced.

**Kit Hinkle:** We have been wrestling with a tough subject this week. But is it possible to even explain the bad things in our lives? Let's see what Kit has to share today.

Never do I try to explain why bad things happen to good people. **God is God and we cannot argue with His power, His authority, and His goodness.** Painful circumstances can break our resolve to have faith in God, break our spirit of hope, and break our courage to continue on. **But it's in painful circumstances that we can grow to depend on Him to hold us together.**

He forms us into His image of perseverance. United with His strength, we become unbroken. In our flesh, we are weak. But in His immensity, God is strong. He bolsters us up when, in our frail faith, we lean on Him. It's that resolved spirit that shines through you when He brings you to your next steps with vigor and life. Just hold fast to the exhortation in *Isaiah 41:10*, *"… fear not, for I am with you; be not dismayed, for I am your God; I will strengthen you, I will help you, I will uphold you with my righteous right hand."* Isaiah tells us not to recoil in fear when life gets at you.

Let us trust and stand firm! Amen

## <u>May 16</u>

### Fear with the Force of Many Waters

By Ami Atkins

"What if something happens to him?"

My friend's voice broke, her tears flowed. Fear. Anxiety. Unknowns.

We put our hands on her and prayed that test results would come back negative. We prayed for God's protection. But we also affirmed that God is good even if He chooses not to heal.

We prayed for peace, rest, and calm hearts. We prayed that ultimately God would be glorified, that He would use this circumstance for the sake His kingdom.

My own tears formed. Empathy was deep in that moment, and I understood the struggle. Her words took me back to when I asked the same question. I thought of the journal entries.

I thought of all the journal entries I had written.

Following the first trip to the ER, my husband and I had a time of overwhelming tenderness and affection. I remembered my husband pulling me into a bear hug as he said, "I just love you so much. I can't even contain how much I love you. I just want to be near you and never let you go." Jon was always lavish in his affection, but these days were radically sweet.

I sat with my coffee and Bible in hand, having time with God while Jon slept in. Anxiety trickled at first. But then the dam broke, **slamming me with the force of many waters**. *Oh God, what if You're giving us this sweet time because something is going to happen to him?*

At that point, there was no reason for me to consider that he would die. The question was born

175

solely out of fear. I was reminded of the Scripture that says *'perfect love casts out fear.'* I prayed, *You are perfect love. I don't want to even imagine facing death, but I know You would give grace. I will love him and cherish him as long as You allow me to, but Jon is Yours. Oh, Father, I need your help! Please cast this fear from me.* And He did.

*"Fear not, for I have redeemed you; I have called you by name, you are mine. When you pass through the waters, I will be with you; and through the rivers, they shall not overwhelm you; when you walk through the fire you shall not be burned, and the flame shall not consume you. For I am the Lord your God, the Holy one of Israel, your Savior!...You are precious in my eyes, and honored, and I love you." Isaiah 43:1-4 NIV*

Jon died a week later. Though my mind had flitted to death, it still came unexpectedly. No one thought he would die.

Tonight I asked God to protect my friend from this path. Our God is big, and He is able to do abundantly above what I can ask or think. He is able to heal.

However, with confidence I could say, "**No matter what,** God is still good. He is big enough when fear hits with the force of many waters."

This God was with me. This God carried. Even now, my cup runs over.

And if her biggest fear becomes reality, this God will carry my friend also.

*This article in its entirety can be found on our website www.anewseason.net

## May 17

### A Matter of Semantics

Liz Anne Wright

> *Brothers and sisters, I do not consider*
> *myself yet to have taken hold of it.*
> *But one thing I do:*
> *Forgetting what is behind*
> *and straining toward what is ahead,*
> *I press on toward the goal to win the prize for which God*
> *has called me heavenward in Christ Jesus.*
> *Philippians 3:13-15 NIV*

**Are you ready to move on?**

Have you heard this, sisters? Sometimes the (usually) well-meaning person means "past the grief".

This may be a simple question, but, to me, the meaning, and its implications, is far from simple.

Hmmm...*move on?* Frankly, I have trouble with those words. "Move on" signifies, to me, a cleaving of the past—permanently. Nope. Not there. Not sure I ever will be. Not sure I ever *want* to be.

But what should we call it?

When my sweet husband, the love of my life and father of my children, departed early for Heaven, I *couldn't* be married to him any longer.

But move on?

I prefer *move forward.*

I am still me - very much alive and trying hard to continue to live in this world instead of longing for things that are no longer mine to have.

And by God's grace, I *can*!

I *can* move forward, past those who don't understand this grief and give them grace anyway. I *can* move past the sadness and the pain into what the

Lord has for me in this new season of my life. I *can* be a good mother to my children by leaning on God. I *can* choose to love again, should the Lord will it.

I can move past those who don't understand who I am and where I am--holding onto what was beautiful and wonderful about my life with Keith, yet changing and adapting as I need to for this new life without him.

And, even when the battle is wearying, God is there. He has my back, and loves me more than I could ever imagine.

I can't help but think of the words to the old hymn, *Great Is Thy Faithfulness.* If you aren't familiar, you can type it into the computer and hear many arrangements. Listen closely to the words.

As you "move forward" in your new life, Sisters, I pray you can cling to this truth: **God loves you more than you can imagine, no matter what you call it**.

*Dear Father, I pray that I am not bogged down by the words of this world - what they call my grief, what they call my life - but can look always to the Word of Truth that comes directly from You. In Jesus' Name, Amen.*

## May 18

## White-Out Faith

By Jill Byard

*She is not afraid of snow for her household,*
*for all her household are clothed with scarlet.*

*Proverbs 31:21 ESV*

White on white, set in a background of more white, throw in a steady wind, temperatures below zero and you have the makings of a good ol' northern winter blizzard. I found myself smack in the middle of this scenario during a six hour road trip. Two hours away from home and the visibility was almost non-existent; turning around wasn't safe. I was feeling extremely anxious about what I was going to encounter as I kept moving ever so slowly forward. The only thing I knew for sure was I had to move, that sitting still wasn't safe. So, I called out in my uncertainty "Lord, please protect us on our travels. Help us!"

As I was inching along the snowy stretch of highway, I realized there was a spiritual lesson about my journey in grief in the midst of the white-out swirling around me.

While in the midst of this long white-out-- when I realized that it wasn't even safe to turn around and go back the way I had come--I realized that I would have to go straight through it, and that slowly was probably the safest way to proceed. I couldn't just stop moving or turn around. And that's how it is with grief. We do not want to walk through it, but we must. We can't turn back because it's not healthy. The safest way is to keep moving forward.

The long day of traveling in blizzard conditions made my eyes hurt. I kept straining them to try and catch a glimpse of what was ahead, but it was impossible because the white was all around me. If I thought about what was ahead, I would worry more. I had to stay focused on the moment, focused on the present. I had to seize it in order to keep making progress.

So it is with the future and my grief journey. The further out into the future I look, the harder it is to find peace. It's overwhelming that I definitely can't see up ahead, around curves, or over hills. But I have to stop worrying about what is too far ahead and focus on the right now. I have to trust that as I move further in my journey, He will continue to equip me with the abilities I will need to get around the curves or to the top of the hills.

As I kept moving down the road, it was difficult to even detect where exactly the road was. I began relying on the rumble strips or chatter bumps to help guide me in my lane.

I am so thankful that God is even better than those rumble strips or chatter bumps on this grief road. Sometimes when grief swirls around me and I am smack in the middle of one of its white-outs, His voice and His Truth guide me like the rumble strips encouraging me to keep moving forward no matter the pace. He sees what is beyond the now and He has it covered. Chatting with Jesus out loud helps keep me stay in the center. It was a necessity as I was traveling, and it is a complete necessity as I make my way through the storms on this grief journey. My traveling would be even slower if I ventured out on my own. I know, I have tried it and I end up in a bank of deep despair that will need more than a tow truck to get me out.

*Dear Lord, please help me cry out to You in the midst of my grief. Help me remember to cling to the knowledge You have my future in the palm of Your hand. Thank You for the work You are going to do on my behalf in my present and my future. You are great and worthy to be praised. In Your Mighty Name, Amen.*

## May 19

## Four Strong Corners

By Linda Lint

*Man shall not live and be upheld and sustained by bread alone, but by every word that comes forth from the mouth of God.*
*Matthew 4:4 (Amplified Version)*

When we married, I brought with me the delight of assembling jigsaw puzzles. It quickly became a hobby we enjoyed together. We could spend hours, and sometimes days, putting together a large, complicated puzzle. We had a routine - first sorting through all the pieces to find the edges and corners, then proceeding to fit together the remaining pieces based on that framework - and having the reference picture on the box helped a lot! Occasionally, we would get side-tracked and attempt to assemble the puzzle without the frame being in place. We found this was never really successful and led to frustration and wasted time. He made frames for them and they still hang throughout our home. I treasure them.

Every once in a while, we would end up with a piece missing after the puzzle was completed. Sometimes, it was a body piece. Sometimes it was an edge or even a corner piece. It seemed we could overlook the missing body piece but the absence of that edge or corner piece was very apparent and the puzzle was useless for framing.

I still love to assemble puzzles. However, due to space limits and a very "helpful" cat, I now assemble the puzzles online. The process is the same, however. First, the corners and edges - then the rest. Occasionally the site offers a "challenge" puzzle to assemble with just a title - no reference picture. It is pointless for me to attempt assembly without the corner and edge pieces in place. The puzzle frame is the only reference I have to continue.

While I was working on the most recent challenge, I was thinking how my life now is similar to the "challenge" puzzle experience.

I have in front of me a large group of puzzle pieces. I have a title "Linda's life now without her husband". I must work on getting this puzzle together. It is the corner and edge pieces that will give me a strong start - a solid foundation in putting this picture together.

My four strong corners come straight from God's Word: (New Living Translation)

*When I have trouble sleeping: Psalm 4:8 "In peace I will lie down and sleep. For You alone Lord God cause me to dwell in safety."*

*When storms blow in: Proverbs 15:25 "The Lord tears down the house of the proud, but He protects the property of widows."*

*When I am concerned about repairmen and business dealings: Deuteronomy 10:18 "He ensures that orphans and widows receive justice".*

*When I miss my husband and need to talk:* Isaiah 54:5 *"For your Creator will be your husband; the Lord of Heaven's Armies is His name. He is your redeemer, the Holy One of Israel, the God of all the earth".*

These four strong corners anchor the framework of my life now - and a truly solid anchor it is. It will take the remainder of my days to complete this particular "challenge" puzzle. But, that's ok - because the corners and edges are solid and I have the promise of God's Word that when the last piece is in place I will be joining Him in Heaven!

*Father:, Your Word is my life. It sustains me and gives me strength. I know I can rely on it totally to guide me through this life-time assembly process. I am so very grateful.*

## May 20

## What Does He Want?

By Bonnie Vickers

> *"The Lord is my portion," says my soul,*
> *"therefore I will wait for Him."*
> *The Lord is good to those whose hope is in Him,*
> *to the one who seeks Him.*
>
> *Lamentations 3: 24-25NKJV*

It started out as a simple trip to the grocery store. Six weeks had passed since my husband's home-going, and I could not postpone the trip any longer. I had to get some food in my house.

I carefully made my way through the produce section. It seemed safe enough. I even managed to make it up and down a few aisles. *So far, so good*, I convinced myself. But, as I rounded the corner and my eye caught the display of cereals, the melt down began. I struggled for air. And slowly the tears began to fall. My mind took me back to the previous shopping trips and I realized then how they were centered around my husband. What would <u>he</u> want for dinner? What kind of cereal would <u>he</u> want? What would <u>he</u> want?

Overcome with emotions, I fled from the store. Thankfully, by God's grace, I have grown quite a bit since that grocery store melt down. Facing this new season of my life with hope and keeping my eyes focused on the cross, my question has now changed to "What would **HE** want?" What would **GOD** want?

Isn't it wonderful that He has given us a guidebook for instruction? His Word tells us what He wants, and by delving into it, we can discover not only what He wants for our lives, but what He has in store for our lives.

What does **He** want?

He wants us to know **He** loves us. *Because your loving-kindness is better than life, my lips shall praise You. Thus I will bless You while I live; I will lift up my hands in Your name. (Psalm 63:3-4 NKJV)*

He wants us to know **He** will comfort us. *You shall weep no more. He will be very gracious to you at the sound of your cry; When He hears it, He will answer you. (Isaiah 30:19NKJV)*

He wants us to know **He** is with us. *The Lord will guide you continually, and satisfy your soul in drought, and strengthen your bones; you shall be like a watered garden, and like a spring of water, whose waters do not fail. (Isaiah 58:11NKJV)*

He wants us to know **He** will help us. *Our soul waits for the Lord; He is our help and our shield. For our heart shall rejoice in Him, because we have trusted in His holy name. (Psalm 33:20-21 NKJV)*

He wants us to know **He** hears our cries. *In my distress I called upon the Lord, and cried out to my God; He heard my voice from His temple, and my cry came before Him, even to His ears. (Psalm 18:6 NKJV)*

He wants us to know **He** has a plan. *For I know the plans I have for you, declares the Lord, plans to prosper you and not to harm you, plans to give you hope and a future. (Jeremiah 29: 11 NIV)*

Sisters, I know this journey is hard. But, if we trust Him - we can discover His plan for this new life we are in. Even as we walk it without our beloved husbands by our sides.

As **He** cheers me on - I can imagine my husband cheering me on as well. He would be proud that I am moving forward.

We lived abundant lives with our husbands. We can now live it without them.

After all, it is what **He** wants.

*Heavenly Father, please keep my heart and thoughts focused on Your will for this new season of my life. Thank You for Your Word, where I can be assured of Your love and concern for me. Amen*

## May 21

### I Have a Story to Tell

By Karen Emberlin

> *So encourage each other and build each other up,*
> *just as you are already doing*
>
> *1 Thessalonians 5:11NLT*

They say "opposites attract" and that was certainly the case for us. My husband was a leader and I was very content to be a follower. I was always content to let him speak (for both of us) and stay in the background. He was not shy, like I was!

However, I seem to be changing since losing my husband. Even though it is not my nature, I believe the Lord has been urging me to "speak out" and tell my story – a story of how He walks with me and gives me the courage to take each step to move forward on this journey.

I am finding the pain of this journey gives me an opportunity to trust Him more, and it draws me closer to Him. Even joy can emerge from the ashes of this adversity through trusting and thanking Him.

My unexpected journey of widowhood began on 1/2/12. In just the week before, my husband and I had celebrated Christmas, our forty-eighth wedding anniversary, and then spent a quiet New Year's Day at home. That evening everything seemed very normal as we prepared to settle in for the night. I had difficulty sleeping, so after keeping my husband awake from tossing and turning, I decided to go to my recliner and at least let him rest. We talked and he agreed that was a good idea. Again, no warning that anything was wrong. I finally fell asleep in my recliner and woke up a few hours later to find that my husband had passed in his sleep sometime during those few hours. What a shock! I will never forget the feeling of panic that set in as I realized he was gone! I depended on him for everything and could not even imagine how I could ever survive and go on without him.

In less than a month after my husband died, I left our home, most of our earthly possessions, our church and our friends and moved several hundred miles to live with family. After a year, I downsized again and moved back to the area where I was raised. I had been gone from there for over forty years, but felt it offered the stability I was looking for in this season of my life. During the second year, I went thru three surgeries and continue to live with daily health issues. All of which were things I thought I could not do without my husband by my side!

Even though my whole world was turned upside down, because of God's grace, *I have survived!*

The past thirty-three months have not been easy and certainly not my choice. There are chapters of my story I would rather not include. As I go back and read the things I have written, I sometimes feel like I focus on the pain and loneliness too much, nevertheless, it is real and a vital part of my story!

However, because I believe and trust my heavenly Father, I will humbly attempt to accept this part of my story and move forward knowing that He always has my best interest in His heart and plans.

Yes, I have a story to tell – one that began when I took my first breath and it will not end until I breathe my last. I don't know what the rest of my story will be – but God does. He has the storyline already figured out and is carefully crafting the words and happenings to fill in the blanks. It's up to me to keep moving forward, no matter how slowly, in order to see what the rest of the story is.

One never knows who might be influenced by our words or actions, so, it's also up to me to keep telling my story. I want to encourage others that they too can survive on this journey, and even find joy again!

*Heavenly Father, I thank You for walking with me on this lonely journey and giving me the courage to move on. I pray that each time I share my story with others, You might allow even one to find encouragement and not give up! Let me never forget You are there for me – always. Amen*

## May 22

## Widow Brain

By Kit Hinkle

*Praise the Lord; praise God our Savior!*
*For each day He carries us in His arms.*
*Psalm 68:19 NLT*

I remember that feeling, just weeks after I lost Tom. My four little boys and I walked about in a fog—playing and living life normally in some moments—collapsing with emotion the next. The range of emotion is so wide—and yet each one so normal. I want to share just one aspect of my grief experience a few weeks out that might help you—my *widow brain*. Have grace with yourself in the coming months. It all feels like a blur, so don't be surprised if you forget appointments or conversations.

One afternoon a month after my loss, I took my little boys to a pet shop. The featured pet of the day—baby bunnies. Dozens of them—all out in an open pen for anyone to hold. My ten year old cradled one in his arms, a genuine grin spreading over his face. It was the first long-lasting smile I saw on him since his father tossed him in the air at the swimming pool, just weeks before. "Mom, can we stay here a while, so I can hold every one of these bunnies?"

How could I resist? It was so wonderful seeing him smile like that. Bunny after bunny got a bit of his loving. As I watched him, I felt the Lord's comfort reassuring me, *he will be okay.* I was completely immersed in the moment.

My cell phone chirped. "Kit?"

I recognized the voice. She was not only a lovely woman from my church—she happens to be the president of a world-wide women's ministry. I quietly wondered why she was calling. We were acquainted, but not particularly close. Something nagged at the back of my mind.

"We are at your front door. Are you home?"

The nagging thought revealed itself—they had scheduled to bring me a meal!

Heat rose at the back of my neck as I looked over at Brian, lost in bunny mania, and calculated a twenty-five minute drive back to my house. Of all people to make this mistake with! She travels practically every week, speaks before thousands, and publishes many books and articles, all while raising a large family of children. And still, she took time to make me a meal!

"Kit?" She asked again.

"Oh," I paused at what to say, and felt the Lord hug me again. "I have to be honest," I said. "My brain left me when Tom did. I forgot. I'm all the way at a pet shop, and I can't get there for another half hour."

Her graciousness helped, but it was up to me to fight the urge to beat myself up. Tears welled up. *I'm not only a lonely widow*, I thought. *Now I've missed out on an evening with a special woman because of my stupid widow-brain.*

"Mom," Brian's squeal of delight interrupted my thoughts. He hugged a little white bunny so close to his face. "These bunnies make me sooooo happy!"

Of course, I wouldn't have put the bunnies before the meeting with her. My *responsible brain* wouldn't do that. What a blessing, though, that God allowed my *widow-brain* to minister to my ten-year-old by putting bunnies first, when my *responsible brain* would have pulled him away from the needed cuddles of comfort.

The grace and mercy from this friend and from the Lord washed over me in an instant, and all of my shame was erased.

She never mentioned the missed meal, and I know why. It's not necessary. That's what grace is about. Isn't it funny how we can do it for others while having such a trial forgiving ourselves?

*Dear Father, grant me the ability to have grace with myself, especially during these first weeks and months after losing my husband. Encourage me that my focus will return, and friends and loved ones will understand when appointments are missed or conversations forgotten. Grant me the focus I need as my daily bread to get me through my grief and safely to the next season in my life. Amen.*

## May 23

## A Bride, a Bird, and an Empty Chair

By Elizabeth Dyer

*Therefore a man shall leave his father and mother*
*and hold fast to his wife, and the two shall become one flesh.*
*Ephesian 5:31 ESV*

This verse was playing and re-playing in my head. I started tearing up as I fixed my hair in anticipation of the evening. Why did it hit me so hard? I texted a friend to ask for prayer to follow through with my commitment.

I was going to attend my first wedding post-Mark, as a widow, re-single. One of 'our' friends was giving their daughter away in marriage.

The first couple I met in the parking lot was one we hadn't seen in several years. They naturally wondered where my husband was this evening. How does one answer the question without making the person feel badly? "Mark passed away in December," I stated flatly. I was quite surprised they hadn't heard. It had been over six months.

This was what I was anxious about as I got ready that morning. I was fearful of those kind of encounters. But I had survived.

The bride was beautiful as she took the hand of her handsome lover in the outdoors of her family's home. I sat there, listening to the ceremony. I was reminded of twenty-one years earlier, making my own declarations of love and dreaming of a long future together. My, how life can send a curve ball.

If I had known then what I knew now, would I have been more excited or less on the day of our wedding? Would I have relished every second of the

Scripture reading or the songs sung? Would I have lingered in our kiss just a second longer? Would I have held his hand just one more moment as I looked into his eyes and pledged my love 'til death do us part?

All these thoughts and more rambled in my head. Thoughts of the bride's future with her new husband, who is too young to be going through cancer treatments instead of his honeymoon. Thoughts of the shaved heads of the groomsmen in solidarity with the groom. Thoughts of the pastor's words about love and intimacy.

Even with all the people *standing* in the back of the ceremony, the chair beside me remained empty. A constant reminder that I *came* alone. I *am* alone. Without my "better half". The chair was a blinking neon sign of my widowhood. Empty Chair. It was difficult to concentrate on much else.

This side of town is full of trees, as opposed to the prairie country on the far west side of the city where I live. Trees mean birds, and as we stood around later, waiting to indulge in the lavish food tables, a bird pooped on the front of my white shirt. Seriously. You can't make this up. I was feeling crummy about the whole wedding thing, then a bird drops his "duty" on me. *Thanks, bird, really. Thanks.* Of all the people there.

I began the day full of anxiety and ended with laughter. God allowed this event because He knew exactly how to get my attention—humor. I needed to lighten up and relax. This first year was going to be full of "firsts", and I felt like God was just reminding me, the year didn't have to be all sadness. Humor was finding its way back into my life, little by little

*Father God, help me see the humor amidst the sadness in my laugh. Thank You for laughter, even on the hard days. Amen*

## May 24

## The Signs of God

By Sheryl Pepple

*He replied, "When evening comes, you say,*
*'It will be fair weather, for the sky is red,' and in the morning,*
*'Today it will be stormy, for the sky is red and overcast.'*
*You know how to interpret the appearance of the sky,*
*but you cannot interpret the signs of the times.*
*Matthew 16:2-3 NIV*

Are you missing the signs of God in your life?

In Matthew 16:2-3, Jesus is warning the Pharisees and the Sadducees not to ask for a sign that He is the Christ. He goes on further to say that none will be given except the "sign of Jonah". Jonah is the sign telling of the resurrected Christ. Today, we have no need of a sign to show that there will be a resurrected Christ. We are, however, frequently blessed by the signs of His presence.

One of my most precious memories is from seven years ago this week. I was on a sailboat in Fiji and I had a close encounter with God our Creator. It started simply enough with an invitation by my husband to watch the sunset together on deck. What happened next was anything *but* simple. Stepping on to the deck, I was immediately struck by sheer awe for the beautiful pinkish/orange sunset, reflecting on the still waters and peeking amongst the majestic mountains. Miraculous beauty in every direction, a panoramic sunset of the most magnificent colors you could ever imagine. It was if I had stepped into Heaven itself. And then suddenly I could not look for an instant more. I ran.

I ran to my cabin. Yanked out my iPod and turned it to the song *Facedown* by Matt Redman, and worshipped with every fiber of my being. It was a moment that became seared in my brain and in my heart forever. It was an epic moment in my life of true worship of our God, the Creator.

Flash forward to this week and I am sorting through sailing pictures to use for my presentation at our Widow's Conference. As I flip through the photographs I am instantly reminded of that moment of worship. A few minutes later I walk to the back of my house just in time to see a beautiful pink sunset. As I stood there gazing at the sunset, I realize for the first time that I have only lived in two homes in my life where I could look out and enjoy the beautiful sunsets. The first was the home I moved into with my two daughters after the death of my first marriage, and the second is the home I recently moved to after the death of my beloved husband. Suddenly, my heart floods with gratitude for the God who makes Himself known through His creation. How did I miss the sign? He never leaves us nor forsakes us. We are never alone.

This journey of grief can feel so lonely at times, and it is easy to get trapped by our fears. Sometimes, it can feel like the storm will never end. But even in the midst of the storm, **God is with us**. The signs are all around us. He is our creator and we are precious to Him. He is working all things together for good. He is faithful and most importantly, He loves us.

*Dear Heavenly Father, thank You for Who You are! Your Presence in my life is a gift beyond compare! Help me see the signs of Your Presence in my daily life. Let others see You through my life, so they may come to know You and believe in You. Amen.*

## When I Long To Be Held By Human Arms

By Ami Atkins

The room was cold.

"Oh, well, better cold than hot for sleeping."

I crawled into bed, bringing the covers snuggly to my nose, leaving only eyes exposed to the elements. My feet quickly cocooned themselves in the down comforter. I lay on my side, knees bent, arms clutching a pillow. Everything was customary. But something was wrong. It took me a minute, but then I remembered; I was on my left side.

*"Quick, Lovee, huddle for warmth!"*

*His strong arms circled me, his knees tucked behind mine. He held me close, heat radiating against my back from his very solid, very physical presence. He prayed aloud. There was security. We lay that way for a while, content.*

*"Okay, switch."*

*He rolled over, and I turned also, both of us now on our right sides, my knees tucked behind his knees. I held him close. And he was asleep within seconds, his chest rising and falling in a slow, gentle rhythm. I nestled behind him, warm and secure.*

*Night after night we followed this pattern. He held me for a while. Then I held him. Then he fell asleep. And I lay there soaking in his warmth, taking in every detail. Finally I slept.*

But I have not started the night on my left side for almost two years. Perhaps it hurts too much to imagine him there behind me, knowing the reality that he's not. Who am I kidding? It hurts regardless which side I face! I guess last night, however, realization hit me square in the eyes; what used to be such an integral part of my life, no longer feels customary.

As I lay there on my left side, I welcomed the sorrow. Sometimes that's an okay thing. Sometimes it's a necessary thing. Nobody tells you that grief even affects the side upon which you sleep.

*"Lord, how long must I be alone? Please be near me. Help me know the security of Your presence when I long to be held by human arms."*

As I continued to pray, peace flooded in, remarkable and true. I was warm and secure. I knew the very real presence of the Lord; God was near. Sleep was not an unwilling guest that lingered in the shadows. Rather, it came sweetly, and I drifted off without turning over.

I have learned much about dwelling in the presence of God. Let me say it this way: I have learned to be aware. Tragedy and grief taught me to run to Christ, to slow down, to listen, to hear His voice echo from the pages of His Word, to know the comfort of the Holy Spirit, to know that my heart and mind can be guarded with incomparable peace. (Philippians 4:6)

Likewise, prayer has become a continuous, flowing conversation. I'm learning to talk to God through the mundane: showering, driving, folding laundry. And I'm learning to talk to Him when my heart is filled with sorrow. Or anger. Or fear. It's totally safe because I have a great High Priest who intercedes for me.

Through Jesus, I have unlimited access to the Father, and I can run to Him with any emotion. He is big enough.

*"For we do not have a high priest who is unable to sympathize with our weaknesses, but one who in every respect has been tempted as we are, yet without sin. Let us then with confidence draw near to the throne of grace, that we may receive*

*mercy and find grace to help in time of need." Hebrews 4:15-16 ESV*

Therefore, I may come boldly. I can expect grace. I can expect mercy. To be near Him, is to be in His very presence.

Yet it is not every night that I welcome peace so easily. Sometimes, I must wrestle. Sometimes I must cry out. Sometimes the longing for human touch seems much more real than the presence of God.

I don't pray perfectly. But I have Someone who does. When I long to be held by human arms, He reminds me that His arms are stronger, His security infinite. He holds me close. The safety He offers is far beyond what my husband had the ability to give.

He is near.

## May 26

### Conversations

By Kit Hinkle

*The serpent was clever, more clever than any wild animal God
had made. He spoke to the Woman: "Do I understand that
God told you not to eat from any tree in the garden?"
The Woman said to the serpent, "Not at all. We can eat from
the trees in the garden. It's only about the tree in the middle of
the garden that God said, 'Don't eat from it; don't even touch
it or you'll die.'"*

*Genesis 3:1-3 (The Message)*

In my reading of Genesis this morning, I was
struck by how quickly Eve got trapped by the serpent's
conversation. Before she even knew it, she herself
wasn't speaking what she knew was truth about what
God really told her about the forbidden fruit. Why did
she let herself get into that conversation in the first
place?

Then I thought about times in the years
without my husband Tom when I've started an anxious
cycle of self-talk, leading me to further unrest. I
wonder sometimes how I got on that dialogue with
myself in the first place, and then I wonder, was I
having the conversation with me or with the enemy
himself?

Eve's first mistake was to engage in a
conversation with the serpent. How many times has
the devil lured a widow into those conversations where
he flusters her, twists her up in her own thinking, until
she buys into his lies. What are yours? How about
these...

I can't go to church alone.
I can't fix a faucet.

I can't remember to take the trash out—that was my spouse's job.

My kids will always be at a disadvantage without a father.

There's no one else who will ever be good enough to spend the rest of my life with like my spouse was.

Married couples only want to socialize with other couples—no one wants to hang out with a widow.

I can't manage my finances alone.

It would be selfish to do things for myself—my kids need me.

Do you know what to do when you're in a conversation with a serpent? I have learned to recognize who I'm tangling with, and I let God prepare my response. I've learned to keep my conversations on Godly truths brief and straight from God's Word, just as Jesus did. Each time Jesus was tempted in the wilderness, He answered with, "It is written."

We can recognize the danger of letting the enemy worm his confusing thoughts and negativity in our hearts and stop him before he gets a chance. Arm ourselves with spiritual truths and reverse the lies. Yes, God will introduce me to new people at church so I won't be alone. Yes, anyone can fix a faucet if they clear their minds and take it one step at a time. Yes, taking out the trash is my responsibility, and God hasn't given me more than I can handle.

*Father God, please help me learn how to reverse satan's lies and turn to You only. Encourage me to talk over my worries with You and let Your Truth reign in my heart. Amen.*

## May 27

## Allowing God to Love You

By Julie Wright

> *You're blessed when you feel you've lost*
> *what is most dear to you.*
> *Only then can you be embraced by the One most dear to you.*
>
> *Matthew 5:4 MSG*

With the recent passing of my uncle just a few weeks ago, a new flood of emotions fell upon my heart. I knew how hard the days, weeks and months ahead would be for my aunt and the family, especially after forty-four years of marriage. To faithfully be by his side through all the ups and downs of his all too brief battle with cancer. What a testimony of love that is!

The feelings of sadness gave way to some hope in knowing that my uncle was no longer suffering in his earthly, cancer ridden body. Hope in the knowledge that one day I will join him and others in heaven forever…rejoicing and praising God with all our might. Hope in knowing our earthly time is short compared to the eternity we will spend in heaven.

Then the hope gave way to endless tears that fell harder and harder the more I let my "feelings" get the best of me. Tears that fell for all the moments that would no longer be shared together. Tears for all the holidays, birthdays and milestones of our children that he can longer celebrate with us. Tears for all the decisions, changes, and future endeavors that need to be made without him.

That's when I realized that I can't let my *feelings* get the better of me. I can't allow them to cloud my judgment of how God truly "feels" about me. Our emotions are so raw and flippant in the early stages of grief. I remember telling everyone that "I'm fine. Really, we're all fine," knowing that if they followed me home and plucked the roof off to peek inside, they would find me curled in the fetal position crying on top of our bed. I bet they wouldn't think I was "amazing, so God-centered, and strong" at that point.

But regardless of how we are truly *feeling* or how we may *interpret* the feelings we have for God, the **truth** is He loves us. Even when He's taken the one person who is most dear to us on this earth, He loves us. It's in that time that we can start to feel loved and embraced by God and begin to move towards those feelings of hope, wholeness and love again. One painful step at a time...

Allow God to love you through friends, strangers, your church, your family, and your emotions. The good ones and the bad ones. He created us. He knows how we really feel. Don't mask it or pretend your feelings aren't allowed. Emotions are a healthy outlet of our pain. Let them flow.

Allow God to love you. Period.

That is when you will begin to *feel* whole again; when you are embraced by the One who is most dear to you.

*Heavenly Father, meet me where I am. Feelings of sadness, loneliness, and grief or even in the feelings that say,* I'm okay. I've got this. *You are the One who will embrace me tightly and get me through the deepest, darkest valley to the other side. You are the One who can love me with an everlasting love. Amen.*

# May 28

## Can We Talk?

By Jill Byard

> *Each time He said, "My grace is all you need.*
> *My power works best in weakness."*
> *So now I am glad to boast about my weaknesses,*
> *so that the power of Christ can work through me.*
> *2 Corinthians 12:9 NLT*

As I study and seek out God's will for my life, this verse always meanders in and sits for a spell in my quiet time. I'll be honest, it has always baffled me. I mean "boast about my weaknesses?" I would prefer it said, "hide your weaknesses and never talk about them."

**Isn't it like Jesus to flip this thinking of ours around on us?**

We want to brag in our strengths and our accomplishments. We want to pick and choose the best of us for our highlight-reels or our newsfeeds. **This is where Jesus does an impressive back flip on our thinking.** In order to be effective for His kingdom He directs us to not only talk about our weaknesses, but boast in them. The word *boast* has a connection with the word *glory*. The word *glory*, when used as a verb, means to *"exult with triumph"*.

**Why is boasting in our weaknesses so important?**

**Boasting in our weaknesses promotes community.** There is an aspect of vulnerability and an element of humbleness when we choose to talk about our weaknesses. When people hear about my struggles with depression, people-pleasing, or keeping up with housework, they may be encouraged to begin a connection with a sister in Christ, since they have the same struggle in their lives. We can seek Godly solutions together. When we join hands in the midst of our trials, we make community a safe place. Safe places always **acknowledge** struggles, but **look** for solutions and **avoid** operating in shame. That is a direct example from Christ. He always offers solutions when we need correction or guidance. *Accusation and shame come from the enemy.*

**Boasting in our weaknesses points all glory and honor to the King.** We forgo our need to be self-promoters and promote "Him who is able...to accomplish infinitely more than we might ask or think." (Ephesians 3:2- NLT) We let go and let God. When weaknesses are handed over to Him to work through, He is made known. We fulfill our purpose when we make Him known and we help others see the importance of trusting Him with everything.

This road of widowhood definitely makes our weaknesses seem magnified, and we might even discover we have new ones added to our list. It seems overwhelming to think about, but we have His grace in every circumstance. When we shine a light on our weaknesses, Christ promises His power is going to work through us and help us navigate as we encounter struggles. We do not walk alone when we seek to bring our weaknesses into the light. We are doing kingdom work and that has eternal value.

*Dear Father in Heaven, thank You for helping me see the importance of boasting about my weaknesses. Thank You for helping me find a community of believers who looks to You for solutions. Thank You for using every circumstance to make my heap of ashes into a beautiful mountain to shout out Your praises. I want to honor You and make You known in the midst of my heartache. In Your Mighty Name, Amen.*

## May 29

### His Birthday

By Karen Emberlin

> *I thank my God every time I remember you.....*
>
> *Philippians 1:3 NIV*

Since the year I began dating my husband, May twentieth has always been a day for celebration--it was his birthday! Even before we met, that date was celebrated by my Mom and Dad as their wedding anniversary. They were married on the very day my husband was born. He always told me the Lord had it planned!

The first year I was still adjusting to the recent and sudden loss of my beloved and all the changes that were taking place. With the passing of time, I thought I had progressed enough to handle "his day". Our children and grandchildren gathered together for a long week-end to celebrate together. It was a beautiful and memorable time for us to spend together, reflecting on the good times we had shared together with him

The second year, the miles between us did not allow for my children and grandchildren to be with me. But that didn't stop us from remembering "his day." My son and daughter both called to check on me, letting me know they were missing and thinking of their Dad, giving me suggestions on how to celebrate his birthday. My mom, sister and I had dinner and spent the evening together. All in all, it was a "good" day filled with many sweet memories.

As the day came to a close, I began to feel those "waves of grief" starting to roll in yet again! Why? I had experienced a good day and had so many things to be thankful for. Still my heart felt as though it was going to break in two! I wanted so much to give my husband a big "Happy Birthday" hug, tell him how much I loved him, missed him--I just wanted to spend time with him. Nothing I tried seemed to help!

Often times when the waves of grief begin to come, I find sharing my thoughts on paper is a release for me. As I pondered what I could write to relieve the pain, I remembered we had released balloons the first year, sharing our birthday wishes and love to my husband, releasing them toward heaven in the clear blue sky. Some may question the theory of this, but it was comforting for our family to express our loss.

I knew I could not repeat that experience, so I did the next best thing. Going through photos I took of the balloons last year, I chose one as they took flight into the sky. Using that photo, I made my own birthday card and "released" it thru cyber space! The card served as a way for me to release my thoughts to my husband and to a few dear friends who would understand what I was feeling this night. Even though the hour was late, words of encouragement were sent back my direction via the internet.

As I thanked God for the fifty years He allowed me to celebrate this special day with my husband, I began to feel the peace only He can give. He knew all about my feelings.

God was with me just as He promises. And one day, I will be able to celebrate my husband's birthday with him in the splendor of heaven!

I know that there will be more days on this unwanted journey that the waves of grief will return. You, too, may experience days like this – just remember you are not alone! Know that there are other "sisters" walking this same journey who care deeply for you. Best of all, each of us can boldly claim the promises God has given to guide us each step of the way.

*Dear Lord, thank You for being with me on the good days and the ones more difficult. Help me hold the memories and love of my husband in my heart, but not to forget You love me even more than I can imagine and promise to fulfill my every need. Guide and give me strength and healing each day of this journey. Amen.*

## May 30

## Hopeful Grief

By Kit Hinkle

> *But we do not want you to be uninformed, brothers,*
> *about those who are asleep, that you may not grieve*
> *as others do who have no hope.*

1 Thessalonians 4:13 ESV

How is a Christian widows ministry different?

Of course I gave away the answer in the question -- the Christ focus. Have you really thought about why that makes a difference? Why does Christ have to be a part of the grieving process, and can you grieve properly without Christ?

The difference is **hopeful grief**. Hopeful grief recognizes the person who died as having a relationship with Christ and therefore asleep with Him, and the person who remains here as weeping, as Jesus wept when Lazarus died, but with a knowledge that they will be reunited with those who now sleep with Jesus.

Paul explains to the Thessalonians that we are not to grieve without hope. What is this *hopeless grief* that Paul is describing?

Secular ministries comfort, but their support focus is on what we have going on here on earth, while the Christian grief ministries focuses on **eternity and the condition of the soul.**

You can grieve with or without Christ, but the secular ministry comforts the flesh for a temporary salve, while **Christ comforts the soul, for full redemption and relationship with Him**.

I can't say that secular grief support groups don't comfort-- many go to them feel the comfort and encouragement of other people going through similar wounds. The day-to-day loneliness of loss is something we all can relate to, and just hearing that others are going through it allows readers to open up and release their own pain.

And that is what hopeless grief from a faithless support group offers--release of your hurts and feelings. It's positive and helpful, but then what?

It's the "then what" that can make the difference between healing and not healing.

There is talk of rebuilding, of trying to move forward. Of releasing the other person. Of all sorts of imagery about the memory of them lingering, or the person still being part of us forever--but it's all vague. The secular ministry doesn't want to rule out any possibility.

Some faithless ministries will allow the readers to wander into many theories--the dead becoming angels, or visiting us here, or becoming reachable through mediums, or even living in the attic. Some even allow that perhaps the person vanishes from existence altogether--done. No God, no eternity.

Sisters, Christ doesn't want us to grieve without hope. He wants you to cry--to release your tears and share in your sorrow. But **He wants so much more for you**. No matter what your circumstance, or age, or health condition, or level of family responsibility, He wants you to grieve with Hope.

Hopeful grieving is recognizing that we who have experienced death in our families know that everything in this world fades away, eventually. So all you are left with is your relationship with your Creator.

And keeping your eyes focused on that Truth and the eventuality of seeing those who sleep in Christ again--that is what has you willing to move forward alone, serving God's purpose He has for you in the meanwhile.

What is your hopeful purpose here?

## May 31

## A Day to Remember

By Liz Anne Wright

*For I myself am a man under authority, with soldiers under me. I tell this one, 'Go,' and he goes; and that one, 'Come,' and he comes. I say to my servant, 'Do this,' and he does it." When Jesus heard this, He was amazed at him, and turning to the crowd following Him, He said, "I tell you, I have not found such great faith even in Israel."*
*Luke 7:8-9 NIV*

"On behalf of a grateful nation…"

Those dreadfully beautiful words came at the end of my husband's funeral. A young Marine handed me a carefully folded flag. A prayer followed, then a three-round volley, and, finally, "Taps."

Thus began my life as a widow.

Now, I claim no accolades. My husband was long-retired from the Corps when he passed away…an "old guy." He was 49. There are many women who have suffered more, losing their loves on the battlefield, gone in an instant in a far-away place. I do not know the pain of the dress uniform coming to the door with the news.

But I stand proudly as a military widow…especially this time of year.

My husband is buried in a national cemetery. It was his wish, even written into his will. Each year at Memorial Day, we honor him, and others who have served, by attending the ceremony at the cemetery. It is a special day, but not especially easy.

We always bring supportive friends with us to the ceremony. Some are fellow military families, who snap to attention as the flag comes by and the National Anthem is played. My heart breaks a little at the beauty of it and at the memory of Keith doing the same.

We purposely bring *others* to the ceremony also, those who are not military, who may not understand the reason why families live that life, putting themselves in harm's way for others. They are touched, and we are blessed to be sharing such a tender but important part of our lives.

I have met other widows at this ceremony as well, sisters on this journey. We are broken at that point, having just seen a reenactment of sorts of the end of our husbands' funerals, hearing again the volley and the bugle. We meet, say, "I'm sorry," and watch each other with a thousand emotions in our eyes, *knowing* what it feels like. Connections are made, beautiful and poignant. Strangers hug, share a tear, and go on. It is a very powerful, but raw, day.

But absolutely worth it.

God has given my family a mission. We are the keepers of the testimony of the life of my husband-- the man he was, and the God he served. We are bound by a duty to both that man and that God to share this testimony for God's greater purpose and glory. It is not an amazing testimony, but just an ordinary one. A Godly man got sick and died. No great hero; just a servant.

We try to further the cause of Christ in our little corner of the world by remembering those who have given their all. But don't we all have that responsibility?

God has given *each of us* a mission in life. We make choices to follow that path toward Him or away from Him. And in this widow walk, I am so thankful for this Commander who directs my path and my steps, who loves me more than I can measure.

For I stand proudly in the army of the Lord. And if He tells me to go, to share, to walk this walk, I am willing to do so. His ways are best. Amen and amen!

*Father, I stand amazed when I see what You have done in me and through me on this journey. It is the hardest thing I have ever done by far. But to be a part of the little moments when I can touch others by walking in Your ways, following Your orders and lead, yet it brings a joy I have not known. It humbles me to know that You can use me, use this time, as something beautiful. Help me to always see what You would have me do, and to touch the people You would have me touch. In Jesus' name, Amen.*

# Index of Authors and subjects

# Connect With Us!

We hope you enjoyed these daily devotions. We have more ways to connect with A Widow's Might/aNew Season Ministries:

- **Social Media**:

  Twitter      @anewseas
                  @AWidowsMight

  Facebook   aNew Season Ministries
                  A Widow's Might

- **Website:**

  www.anewseason.net

- **Conference:**

  Check website for latest details!

- **Retreats:**

  Ruth Training Retreats

- **Blogs:**

  Be a Guest Blogger – Check website for details!

- **Prayer Requests:**
  Submit on our facebook page or on our website!

## Also Available:

Available for purchase through Amazon.com

Summer Edition

Autumn Edition

Winter Edition

## Our Hope

You can see hope in a woman's demeanor. She has shed the chains of fear and anxiety, and she's welcoming the future.

And you can feel it in her conversations. That's why you feel the smiles in the heart of each of our writers – no matter what difficulties she has had to endure or still endure in her life. The smile still shows up, because it's the smile of Hope.

Every woman has a different background. Some have gone to church, some have not. We get that, and choose to open the door to you, regardless of your past circumstances. We're about your growth and healing and believe that both must come from a personal relationship with Jesus.

He is our only true Hope. Church is not our salvation. Neither is being a good person. We are given the gift of eternal life because of how much God loves us, not because of what we can do.

Each of us on our team knows what it's like to stumble or completely mess up in life. Just ask us – we'll tell you. Each of us has had life circumstances hurt us so badly that we begin to wonder, *Is it something I did?* Deep down, we know we're not perfect, but the condemnation we sometimes feel can prevent us from the complete and miraculous healing that should be ours through Him.

We alone can't save ourselves – only God can. And He is so merciful that He offers His precious gift of salvation to each of us if we're willing to accept it. He gives us true freedom from our past sins because of what Jesus chose to sacrifice for our sake.

Jesus was God in the flesh, so He never was consumed by selfishness or pride like we are. He lived a perfect life, and then, out of His incredible love for us, He took on the burden of our sin – carrying the weight of all the punishment that we deserved.

That's what the cross is about. It's not just about a good man, martyred for his faith. It's bigger than that. It's like being rescued from drowning by someone willing to dive in and take your place.

(spoiler alert) Remember that scene from Titanic, when Jack drops down into the icy Atlantic waters, knowing it would kill him? He dies so that Rose could live. The idea of someone dying so that another can live shows up in movie after movie. The storyline always draws us because of what it touches so powerfully deep within.

We know that story well because it's what draws us to Jesus. He loves you so much that He took what you and I deserve upon Himself so that we can be free to live our lives out in joy, and then live for all eternity with Him

That drawing close to Jesus is our joy. There is only one way for us to be saved, and that's through His dying for us.

God's promises are true: All we need to do is believe in Him, and we will be saved. When we pray and ask Him into our hearts, He saves us. We pray by saying, *"I know I've sinned. I've hurt others, and I can't seem to be what I should be. I'm sorry, God, and I admit I need You. I surrender my will to Yours, and I will trust You and walk with You."*

Once you do that, you are His forever, and no one can steal that salvation from you! But, the promise doesn't end there. Once you have salvation, you can build joy in your new season of life, no in relationship with Him, and with a community of all of us who also endeavor to walk with Him.

Our lives begin anew right now. And, our prayer is that if you have just begun this walk, either as a new believer, or as someone who has renewed her hope in Christ, that you'll let us know by emailing us here.

Blessings to you.

A Widow's Might

38573800R00137

Made in the USA
Middletown, DE
21 December 2016